# Craftland Japan

Uwe Röttgen
Katharina Zettl

# Craftland
# Japan

Foreword by Kengo Kuma
With 583 illustrations

Note on the English writing of names and places: Names in this book are written following the contemporary style of putting first names before family names; historical figures, Tamaki Niime and Chiyozuru Sadahide's workshop names are written in the traditional style. With a few exceptions, including Tokyo, Osaka, Kyoto and Shinto, long vowels, if known, are written as in "Kyūshū" and "Hokkaidō".

Hiroshim

Fukuoka

九州
Kyūshū

沖縄
Okinawa

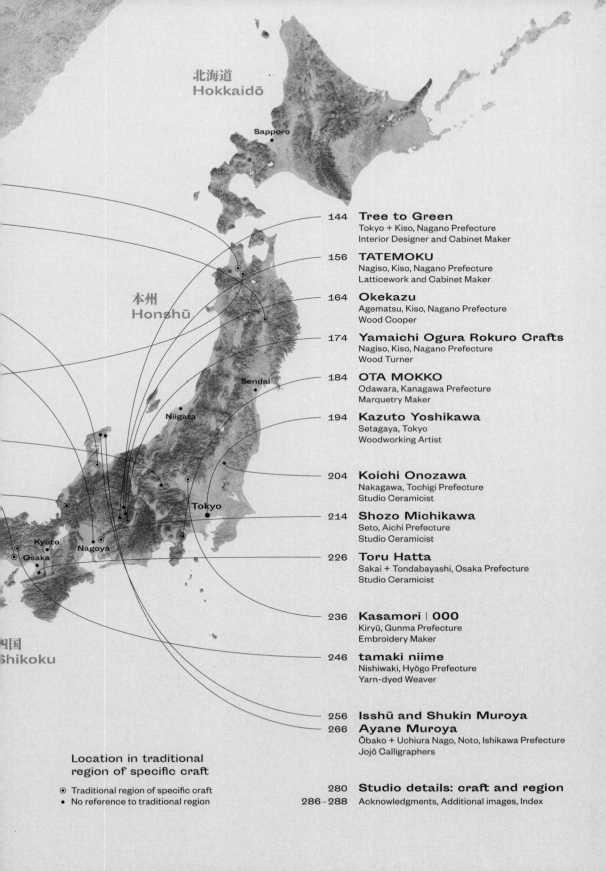

北海道
Hokkaidō

Sapporo

本州
Honshū

Sendai

Niigata

Tokyo

Kyoto
Nagoya
Osaka

四国
Shikoku

Location in traditional
region of specific craft

⊙ Traditional region of specific craft
• No reference to traditional region

# Foreword

When the economic bubble of the 1980s burst and Japan sank into recession during the 1990s, my projects in Tokyo suddenly dried up.

With an abundance of time and nothing to do, I decided to explore Japan and, during my travels, was asked to take on a number of small projects. With all the time in the world at my disposal, I decided to live and work with local craftspeople.

I found skilled and eager craftspeople wherever I went in Japan, however deep into the mountains. After the financial collapse, the government announced that the economy had hit rock bottom and Japan was in crisis. Yet meeting interesting craftspeople in various villages made me feel that Japan was not without worth. I felt that the country had huge potential and that I would be content to continue creating architecture together with the craftspeople of Japan, no matter how small and modest our projects were. Japan's period of recession in the 1990s was known as the "Lost Decade". For me personally, it was the most fulfilling decade of my life and those ten years had a transformative effect on me.

From around the year 2000, I began to work all over the world. I worked in cities and deep in mountainous areas in China, Asia, and Europe, but, in most cases, I was disappointed to find that craftspeople like those in Japan do not exist. I was reminded that Japan's craftspeople are unique and Japan is a unique country.

Why has such great skill developed and passed down through Japan's generations? Perhaps one reason is the country's complex terrain. Even today, seventy per cent of the land is covered by trees, making it one of the most forested countries in the world. The terrain is intricately folded and Japan is a collection of myriad forests, valleys and mountain streams. In each mountain fold, cultures have been protected and close human relationships inherited. Miso and sake are fermented for long periods of time in small containers, just as the skills of Japan's craftspeople have been fermented and honed.

With various soils and climatic conditions existing in each fold of the terrain, this long, narrow country, stretching north to south, is a land of diversity. Japan's forests comprise a wide variety of trees that have been used to create myriad craft products and designs. In these forests, various types of design fermentation took place and a wide variety of flavours and styles were created.

Even after the emergence of a modern Western-style government in Japan, the state was unable to control the diversity of the country's traditional crafts. Even when the government attempted to crush this diversity with concrete and steel, it proved impossible. They could not erode the cultural depth and richness of Japan's mountain folds.

What we should attempt to achieve through architecture and design in Japan is the continued protection of these mountain regions and the restoration of cultural diversity. Japan and its mountain folds conceal a wealth of clues and secrets that will ensure a more sustainable Earth and the survival of humanity.

Kengo Kuma

Kengo Kuma is one of Japan's leading architects and has designed many buildings in Japan and around the world, notably the Suntory Museum of Art in Tokyo, a complex building comprising LVMH boutiques in Osaka, the Besançon Art Center in France, the V&A Dundee design museum in Scotland and the New National Stadium for the Tokyo 2020 Olympics.

# On the trail of virtuoso artistry

There are many ways to approach Japanese craftsmanship. The most immediate is surely to look at and touch the objects themselves, to enjoy the food offered in them, to be enveloped by them, to meet them in Japanese baths, to feel their rough or smooth or soft surfaces.

What skilled hands created these objects? Who are the women and men behind these works, how do they live and work, and what attitudes and dreams do they have?

We wanted to see the hard-working hands of an old master, his much-used tools and instruments, as well as the workshop dust illuminated in the evening sun. We wanted to see handwoven fabrics taking on an indigo colour, and the conversion of plant fibres into delicate paper. We wanted to smell freshly cut cypress wood, to feel the heat of the forge and the sharpness of the blade that arises out of it. A whole cosmos of its own.

The history of Japanese crafts can be traced back through the centuries. Numerous influences from China and Korea have been absorbed with the passing of time, and techniques and styles were further developed and adapted to Japanese needs. Craft objects were often manufactured on behalf of

local lords, under their protection and with their support. Over the course of time, differing regional styles and techniques evolved. The variety of expressions in Japanese ceramics or lacquerware alone is extraordinary.

The most exciting perspective in the workshop of a Japanese master craftsperson is that of an apprentice: observing with curiosity and alertness in order to learn; realizing the intense concentration and care with which each individual work step is carried out; being amazed by tools and techniques, feeling deep joy in understanding correlations. As a book designer and a product designer, this is our personal view of the places where Japanese craftsmanship flourishes, which surprised and amazed us afresh with each new visit.

We initially became acquainted with the craftsmen and women portrayed in this book through their works, which are all devoid of elaborate decorations and attractively modest in form, colour and design. The original materials often remain recognizable, with all their irregularities and peculiarities, such as the characteristic composition of a certain clay, the deformations in the growth of wood or the roughness of the iron. The works want to be picked up, used and thus in some way brought to life. Over time, and with everyday use, their appearance inevitably changes. Discolorations and traces of heat and humidity become visible, and with them the memory of the mutability, imperfection and impermanence of all existence in the world. In most cases, the works follow an aesthetic that has developed strongly in

connection with Japanese Zen Buddhism; they are detached from traditional craftsmanship to a greater or lesser degree, interpreting it in a modern way without ignoring its origin.

With the opening of the country at the beginning of the Meiji period in the nineteenth century, and the incorporation of Western influences into the state and society, Japanese artisans came under growing economic pressure owing to industrialized production, imported goods and changing lifestyles. As a result, various movements emerged, such as the *mingei* (folk craft) movement founded by Sōetsu Yanagi and influenced by the English Arts and Crafts movement, to help hand-crafted objects regain their value and to preserve the old techniques. Since the 1950s, numerous state initiatives, such as the system of distinguishing outstanding master craftspersons as "Living National Treasures", have also contributed to the preservation of this unique landscape of craftsmanship.

Today, there is still a remarkable variety of craft industries, distinctive divisions and styles,* and different ways of working. Furthermore, many artisans and craftspeople work almost exclusively with regional raw materials: they dig and prepare their own clay or they are called into the local forests when trees are cut in order to select the best trunks. In addition to established family workshops, there are numerous small companies, often based in

* DENSAN, the Association for the Promotion of Traditional Craft Industries in Tokyo, currently still lists at least 230 designated Japanese arts and crafts.

the original centres of the respective crafts, as well as countless independently working craftspeople, artisanal designers and artists. Their works are always functional, yet they sometimes seem like art objects too, which is not a contradiction in terms. A separation between applied and "pure" art, between art and craft, did not exist in Japan for a long time, and so we see our protagonists, as they see themselves, rooted in many areas.

In our portraits we show a cross section of different attitudes and approaches within the contemporary landscape of Japanese craftsmanship, away from the craft centres such as Kyoto, Arita and Wajima, which are well known and respected in the West. The craftspeople featured in this book range from the artistically driven and unattached solo artisan to company founders with employees; from masters with apprentices to established and globally exhibiting artists; from the young collective to long-established artisan families traditionally connected to their region and renowned for the highest product quality over many generations. In addition, we are happy to introduce a family of calligraphers, who in their own way reinterpret the traditional art of calligraphy.

They are all impressive characters who pursue their craft professions with dedication, modesty and enormous artistic skill, while at the same time developing progressively and with a clear vision for the future.

Many of the artisans portrayed here began their professional careers as university students in one of the usual business subjects before sooner or later coming into direct contact with craftsmanship. Impressed by the freedom, nonconformity and power of creativity, they consciously decided not to become a "salary man" in one of the bustling, crowded cities, but to live with their families in small towns or in the countryside, with a freely chosen daily routine and more personal contacts, and above all to engage in an activity that would bring them intangible rewards.

In many places there are worries about the future, especially about finding appropriate successors, and yet more and more young people seem to choose this type of working life for themselves.

If you care to, you can learn a great deal from the protagonists. Perhaps the most important thing is to give everything the necessary time. A piece of wood alone needs months or years of attention during weathering; indigo must be cultivated, harvested and processed before it can be used for dyeing; ceramics in wood-fired kilns must be carefully observed for days and nights; *urushi* (lacquer) must rest under precise conditions after each application. Quality in craftsmanship is based on a combination of time, excellent materials, extraordinary skills, care, dedication and refusal to compromise in one's own work.

Despite years of experience, they are all united by the will to pursue lifelong learning and continual improvement, perhaps because perfection also means a state of stagnation. At the same time, they willingly pass on their knowledge and share it with each other. They teach us a more respectful use of resources and remind us to decide more consciously which things we want to surround ourselves with in our everyday life.

To be directly on site seemed ideal to us, with visits lasting several days and allowing us direct contact with the craftspeople and often also with their families. In most cases, the camper, our six-month centre of life and work, was parked just next to the workshops. So we could get to know their daily routine, observe the work steps, explore the surroundings, photograph, film and conduct interviews as close as possible to the events.

Twenty-five times we were welcomed with great kindness and sincerity into a world previously unknown to us, each one as different as the individual personalities who fill these workshops and studios with life. To capture the overwhelming impressions was the motivation behind this book. A holistic insight into the microcosm of contemporary Japanese artisanal craftsmanship, the kind of world that barely exists any more in most industrial nations and which is also increasingly endangered in Japan.

Our path led us away from the usual hotspots, for many thousands of kilometres, down to the rustling bamboo groves on the southern main island of Kyūshū, across the smaller main island of Shikoku on the Seto Inland Sea, to many areas on the main island of Honshū, along its rough coast up to the snow-covered prefectures of Iwate, Akita and Aomori. We watched the cherry blossom come and go, gazed at the moon, enjoyed different types of sake, bathed extensively in Japanese *onsen*, and admired countless sunrises and sunsets. Our journey took us to studios overlooking the Japanese Sea, workshops in the midst of fields, in villages and cities, and stately houses among mountain forests. We went right to the places where Japanese craftsmanship is at home.

Uwe Röttgen, Katharina Zettl

› craftlandjapan.com

"Kawaii ko ni wa
tabi o saseyo."
Let the beloved child
go on its own journey.

Japanese proverb,
cited by Masao Kawahira

# The Artisans

# Nigara Forging

**Uncompromising
pursuit of perfection bears
a sharpened beauty**

二唐刃物鍛造所

Constant rainfall and the last remnants of snow in Aomori have turned the storage space in front of the workshop buildings of Nigara Forging in Hirosaki to soft mud. Despite the family's 350-year history as Tsugaru bladesmiths, their workshop does not have a traditional appearance.

In the annexe where the knife workshop is located, only a few windows let in daylight. A dark grey veil seems to lie over the surfaces of the large forges, mechanical hammers and workbenches. This dim ambience helps Toshihisa Yoshizawa and his son Go to have better control over their forging and so maintain the high quality of their work.

In professional Japanese cuisine, different types of knives are used for different purposes. For example, the *santoku* is used for cutting meat, vegetables and fish, the *yanagiba* for preparing sushi and sashimi, the *deba* for fish in general, and the *usuba* for slicing or chopping vegetables. There are numerous other knives with specialist uses. They differ in shape, length and the way they cut, and sometimes also in the type of steel they are made of. They are all extraordinarily sharp, as can be imagined from the various grinding benches, belt grinders and other sharpening tools in the second workshop room. This is where the knife is honed to its actual function, with the blade sharpened on one or both sides.

Fifth-generation noble swordsmith Kunitoshi Nigara during the Shōwa era.

The principal purpose of a knife as a tool must be to cleanly slice items in the most appropriate way. The main aim in Japanese cuisine is to make the ingredients shine, to bring out their best characteristics. The occasionally uncompromising attitude of Japanese chefs is adopted by the Yoshizawa family at

A testimony by Miyamoto Musashi (1584–1645) hangs on a wall in Nigara's workshop: "In a thousand days of practice, you learn the technique. In ten thousand days of practice, you polish your technique." Miyamoto Musashi was a legendary swordsman, philosopher and founder of the Niten Ichi-ryū style of swordsmanship.

their forges and grinding benches and with their hammers and whetstones. In a way, intransigence becomes their very motivation.

If a knife may be regarded as a work of art – and there are many reasons why it may – Nigara aim to give their products characteristics that elevate them above the realm of craft. One such is the use of specially lacquered handles and sheaths made with *Tsugaru nuri*, the *urushi* lacquerware technique from the same region.

In the ANMON knife series, twenty-five layers of steel are forged to give a ripple effect, inspired by the rippling Anmon Waterfalls of the Shirakami Mountains, a World Heritage Site near Hirosaki. One of the knives of the ANMON series, designed by Kōzō Takeda, is made out of a single piece of steel – both blade and round forged handle – so it does not need a separate handle.

Next to the smithy door hang handwritten notes offering some guiding principles in Japanese. The idiom "God is in the detail", sometimes attributed to Ludwig Mies van der Rohe, is a reminder to do things thoroughly. Another demands that both bladesmiths always give of their best, as the professional users of Nigara knives do in the kitchen. But the most beautiful one says that a heart of iron is also a human heart. The metal should therefore be treated with care, just like a human being, because it is a constant companion as well as the basis for one's livelihood.

二唐刃物鍛造所

I   Snow-covered hills just south of Hirosaki.
II   Go Yoshizawa forms the steel for a high-quality knife on the spring hammer.
III   The bladesmith recognizes the right temperature of about 1,200 °C (2,190 °F) by the way the steel glows.

IV   A light *aideba* knife for fish, from the ANMON series.
V   Forging tongs are the connection between fire, workpiece and bladesmith.
VI   Go Yoshizawa stands in a pit during forging.

VII   The belt grinder fine-grinds the blade.
VIII   Anvils and mechanical spring hammers are grouped around the forge.
IX   Toshihisa Yoshizawa in front of a large sharpening bench.
X   A *yanagiba* knife with *urushi* finishing, from the TSUGARUNURI series.

XI   Hand-forged razor, ANMON knife with lacquer handle, and two letter openers.
XII   A heavy ANMON hunting knife with a blade sharpened on both sides.

Borax powder is used to help forge two
pieces of steel together.

The tang (for attaching the handle) is
hammered into the blade.

A double-sided blade is finished on a
grinding wheel.

吉
澤 **Toshihisa Yoshizawa** is presi-
俊 dent and CEO of Nigara Forging,
寿 a fourteenth-generation family business in Hirosaki, Aomori Prefecture,
making quality knives and steel
construction products. He was
trained from a young age to follow
in the Nigara family tradition as a
bladesmith.

吉
澤 **Go Yoshizawa,** Toshihisa
剛 Yoshizawa's eldest son, will take
over the business one day.

More than 350 years ago, the
ancestors of Nigara Forging were
appointed as armourers to the ruler
of the Tsugaru Domain. Much later,
in the early days of the Shōwa era
(1926–1989) one of their descend-
ants, Kunitoshi Nigara, the noble
fifth generation, distinguished
himself in the production of excellent Japanese swords. During this
period he was recognized as one
of the Living Treasures of Aomori
Prefecture. He passed on his expertise as a bladesmith to Toshihisa
Yoshizawa.

"Actually I hated manu-
facturing when I started,
and even now I'm not all
that fond of it. When I
started my apprenticeship,
I made a lot of mistakes
and I felt I couldn't do
anything right. Every time
I stepped into the work-
shop I was scolded. I
hated working in such a
high-pressure environment.
[...] Craftsmen have to
be good with words, and
they've got to know a lot
about society. Just being
shy, complaining only when
we drink, being pessimistic
about traditional industry
– if we're like that, we're
going to sink our own
ships. That's why I have to
work hard at what I do. [...]
If you work with a men-
tality like mine, even an
uncoordinated guy like me
can enjoy traditional manufacturing." Toshihisa Yoshizawa*

Japan can look back on a
centuries-old tradition of swordsmithing. After the Second World
War, all weapons in the country were
banned and destroyed, and many
swordsmiths had to find an alternative occupation. As one of the few
craft workshops, Nigara Forging
were allowed to continue producing
swords for ritual purposes, which
they did until 1965.

They subsequently transferred
their swordsmithing techniques
and skills to the manufacture of
high-quality knives, and the process
steps remain almost unchanged
today. In this way, the remarkable quality of these hand-forged
Japanese knives is rooted in the art
of sword forging passed down from
generation to generation.

* Quote from an interview with
Toshihisa Yoshizawa by Takafumi
Suzuki for Tokyo Art Beat,
translation by Claire Tanaka.
www.tokyoartbeat.com

Water is always added to the whetstone
when blades are sharpened.

Sulphuric acid is used to make the steel
layers visible.

The obligatory sharpness test with a
newspaper.

# Nigara Forging

二唐刃物鍛造所

**Nigara Forging**

# Suzuki Morihisa Studio

**Iron ore is formed by generations of knowledge, virtuosity**

**Suzuki Morihisa Studio**

鈴木盛久工房

As is typical in Japan, the workshop is located behind a narrow front building that houses the storefront and living areas. Over the years a tree has stretched its crown over the gabled roof of the squat old wooden building. A small turret on the roof serves as a vent for the smoke produced during the various work processes.

Inside, the first thing a visitor notices is the hundreds of moulds in sandy earth tones that are stacked around the edges and in the middle of the room. The smoke-blackened atmosphere is brightened only by fluorescent lights and a little daylight filtering in through the windows. Numerous work tools and raw materials are grouped around the few workstations, which can be recognized only by a flat seat cushion, the semi-finished pots and a single light bulb when the workers – Shiiko Kumagai, the fifteenth-generation Morihisa Suzuki, her son Shigeo Suzuki, and three employed craftsmen – are not in the room.

The almost 400 years of family knowledge and the remarkable craftsmanship of the generations are almost palpable. Hankichi Morihisa Suzuki, the thirteenth generation, was designated an Intangible Cultural Treasure by the Agency for Cultural Affairs, a great honour in Japan. His works were

Hankichi Morihisa Suzuki, the thirteenth generation, left; and Kanji Morihisa Suzuki, the fourteenth generation, with a bust of Hankichi Morihisa Suzuki that he made during his university years.

influenced by tea ceremony, *wabi-sabi* philosophy (a main concept in traditional Japanese aesthetics), but also by modern design. Kanji Morihisa Suzuki, the fourteenth generation, was greatly inspired by Italian design, while the style of the current fifteenth generation is lighter, delicate, and perhaps more feminine. Morihisa Suzuki's son consciously draws his inspiration from urban influences such as architecture, modern art, film and graphics. Thus, while maintaining a consistently high quality, each new generation gives a personal touch to the work in the spirit of the family.

Suzuki Morihisa Studio mainly produces pots for boiling water for the tea ceremony (*chanoyugama*), tea kettles (*tetsubin*) and sake decanters (*chōshi*). It also makes many other beautiful cast-iron products, such as small bowls, chopstick rests, paperweights and more.

In the manufacturing process, which has remained largely unchanged for many years, blades, spatulas and rotation templates are used to design the outer casting moulds. A mixture of very fine sand and binding agents is stacked in the moulds and then dried. Compasses, scrapers, styluses and stamps are used for the laborious manual carving of the finely chiselled patterns and motifs into the dried innermost layer of sand. The art is to visualize the image upside down and reversed at the same time.

During casting, molten pig iron, heated to over 1,300 °C (2,370 °F), is poured into the space between the engraved outer mould and the plain inner mould. Once demoulded, the result is visible for the first time. After deburring and grinding, the kettles are heated in a coal fire to over 1,000 °C (1,830 °F). This creates a layer of natural oxide that protects against rust. Finally, a slightly coloured *urushi* lacquer is applied to the outside of the hot workpiece.

The complexity of the process means that only around twenty kettles are produced per month, and demand is such that the studio's order books are full for years ahead. Water boiled in these tea kettles is enriched with iron particles, something that customers from all over Asia, in particular, highly appreciate.

鈴木盛久工房

I   The traditional workshop at the back of the narrow property.
II   Kettles are heated in the coal fire to create an oxide layer.
III   The moulds are modelled on the ground as long as they do not have a pattern.
IV   The mould half of a lid is prepared with a rotation template.
V   Shigeo Suzuki corrects small details with a hammer and chisel.

VI   Applying *urushi* lacquer to a heated kettle as a finish.
VII   They usually make their own styluses for the detailing of the forms.
VIII   Shigeo Suzuki with pots previously heated in the coal fire.
IX   Miniature altar (*kamidana*) to honour the ancestors and Shinto deities.

X   The details of the surfaces and eyelets are modelled with styluses in the moulding sand.
XI   Detail of a small cast-iron plate with chrysanthemum design.
XII   Morihisa Suzuki in front of hundreds of rotation templates, next to a stack of empty moulds.
XIII   Hankichi Morihisa Suzuki, the famous thirteenth generation, designed these saucers inspired by the Golden

Hall (Konjikidō) in Chūson-ji temple.
XIV   Other small plates, boxes and ashtrays are also made of iron.
XV   *Chagama*, traditional pots for boiling water for tea, are made for classic fireplaces in the ground.
XVI   Cast-iron braziers (*furo*) are also common.
XVII   The finely drawn decorations of an elaborate kettle.

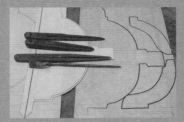

Transferring the cross sections of a new kettle design to rotation templates.

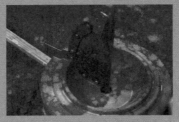

A template is used to prepare the inside of a casting mould.

The inside of the mould is modelled with scrapers and styluses (not pictured).

十五代目 鈴木盛久 **Morihisa Suzuki,** born Shiiko Kumagai, is the fifteenth generation in a family line of kettle casters. She and her son run the Suzuki Morihisa Studio craft workshop for the production of cast-iron teapots and kettles in Morioka, Iwate Prefecture. The eldest daughter of Kanji Morihisa Suzuki, the fourteenth generation, she graduated from the renowned Musashino Art University near Tokyo in 1967.

鈴木成朗 **Shigeo Suzuki,** born Shigeo Kumagai, is the second son of Shiiko Kumagai and serves as president and CEO of the studio. He studied Metal Casting in the Department of Crafts at Tokyo University of the Arts, and worked for several years as a graphic designer, including for his brother's fashion label in Tokyo, before joining the family business in 2008.

The family line of kettle casters was founded in 1625 by Nui Suzuki, a metal caster from Yamanashi Prefecture. Together with Goroshichi Koizumi, a tea kettle caster from Kyoto, he was appointed to cast kettles, bells and cannons

"I grew up around my grandfather, the fourteenth generation, my mother's father. Back then I didn't think my mother would become the next lineage holder. As a child I didn't think I would do this sort of work either; I just came to the workshop to visit and play. My grandfather died when I was ten years old. There was no male heir to continue the tradition and there was indecision about how to proceed. But then, when I was in high school, my mother made the decision and became the fifteenth generation. Our tradition is that this goes from parent to child, so it was when my mother took on the role that I first started to think that my turn would come after her." Shigeo Suzuki

for the feudal lords of the Nanbu clan, who ruled the Morioka region at the time. In the following period, kettles of the Nanbu clan were often presented as gifts in feudal circles. Nanbu ironware (*Nanbu tekki*) soon spread throughout the country and the kettles were used in numerous households because of their excellent quality. Many craft businesses in Morioka still use traditional methods to produce high-quality cast-iron kettles, pans and other utensils.

"I get a lot of inspiration from other types of art like architecture and sculpture, and also from other cultures. I don't really look at past cast-iron things for inspiration. My predecessors were so amazing that if I look too much at their work I get influenced, and it wouldn't be interesting if I just copied their works." Shigeo Suzuki

Liquid iron at 1,300–1,400 °C (2,370–2,550 °F) is poured into several moulds.

The entire outer sides must be deburred.

Finely chiselled motifs can be reproduced on the tea kettles.

**Suzuki Morihisa Studio**

鈴木盛久工房

鈴木盛久工房

# Shimatani Syouryu Koubou

**Euphonious volumes
are created from the flat
through their serenity**

**Shimatani Syouryu Koubou**

シマタニ昇龍工房

The bright, metallic "bing-bing-bing" sound of hammering in Shimatani Syouryu's workshop is almost unbearable without ear protection. Two craftsmen are diligently striking parts of round brass sheets with large hammers, while their colleague works a small silvery shining sheet of metal with precise strokes. The clear marks left by her hammer form the textures of the tinware called *suzugami* (tin paper), whose decorations were inspired by the mystical weather of Japan, with its rain, hail and snow. The actual purpose of the hammering, though, is to compact the metal. The resulting surface design from the hammer is an almost incidental result.

Together with the casting company Nousaku from Takaoka, the Shimatani Syouryu workshop developed the idea of adapting square sheets of hammered tin, available in four sizes, to a given purpose or design. For example, it could be vertically rolled as a vase, waved as a tray, bent up all around as a bowl, or given a raised corner for *wagashi* (sweets served with green tea). After use the thin, pliable sheets are easy to roll flat with the matching wooden stick, before being bent again as desired. The flexible tableware fits perfectly with the passion of the Japanese for perfect presentation.

Despite the physically hard work and high decibel level, the craftspeople seem quite relaxed.

Kumekazu Shimatani and staff members in the main workshop.

This may perhaps be due to the contemplative nature of the activity; the real reason, however, is probably their decades of experience in the production of Buddhist *orin* gongs. Resembling inverted bells, these hammered sounding bowls accompany the meditation and chanting in Buddhist temples.

Each Shimatani *orin* gong is made of three sheet metal parts. The upper ring is hammered from a thick brass strip. This creates

*Orin* gongs in the Sōjiji-soin temple near Monzen, Noto Peninsula.

the characteristic wall thickness that will give the gong's sound stability and fidelity. The middle part, made of thinner brass sheet, is rolled around, welded first to a cylinder and then to the upper ring, and hammered into a bulbous shape. The bottom is made of a circular piece of sheet metal and also has a slight bulge. Only when all three parts have been welded together in a rough bell shape does the base receive its final bulbous form by being repeatedly pushed with its own weight against a round shaping rod.

The harmonious sound of the finished gong is said to have a calming and relaxing effect. The preferred tonality has changed over the decades, while the traditional shape of the bowl remains unchanged. Even smaller gongs resonate for up to thirty seconds when struck with the typical wooden mallet wrapped in leather and rope.

It is only through thousands of hammer blows that the shape of the *orin* is perfected, the sheet metal hardened and the resulting sound made beautiful. The first tone after striking (*kan*) depends on the thickness and density of the metal. Tuning the tones with long and short wavelengths (*otsu*, *mon*) requires a multisensory feeling achieved through many years of training. It enables the master to sense dissonances in the sounding body and to clean them up with targeted hammer blows inside and outside.

シマタニ昇龍工房

I   The workshop is located next to houses in a residential area.
II   Even with heavy hammers, *suzugami* patterns are precisely worked.
III   Tempering is usually done with a gas burner.
IV   Any slight unevenness in *orin* gongs can be seen and corrected only under good lighting.
V   Kumekazu Shimatani compares the sound of two gongs with a beater.
VI   All weld seams must be carefully smoothed.
VII   The sheet metal parts are annealed in a forge.
VIII   Making the hammered upper rim.
IX   The three *suzugami* patterns *samidare* ("summer rain"), *arare* ("hail") and *kazahana* ("dancing snowflakes").
X   Food or other small objects can be perfectly presented on the shiny curved tin.
XI   The brand name is beaten into the metal on a finished *orin* gong.
XII   For the perfect tone, the interior of an *orin* gong is as carefully crafted as the exterior.
XIII   *Orin* gongs in various stages of the making process. Different sizes produce differing sounds.

The upper and middle rings of a small *orin* gong are adjusted.

A medium-sized gong is pushed into shape on the shaping rod.

Two burners heat one *orin* gong to release the tension in the metal.

島谷桼和 **Kumekazu Shimatani,** the representative of Shimatani Syouryu Koubou in Takaoka, Toyama Prefecture, is the third generation of the family business founded in 1909 and specialized in Buddhist singing bowls, or *orin* gongs, and hammered tin goods. They employ about ten specialized staff members. Only he, his son and a third artisan are masters of the whole production process, including the tuning of the *orin* gongs.

島谷好徳 **Yoshinori Shimatani,** the fourth generation, first studied international politics and history in Tokyo and then went on to become a cook. In the end, he decided to follow the family tradition. He learned to make and tune *orin* gongs under his grandfather's guidance for around seventeen years and founded the sub-brand Syouryu for hammered *suzugami* tin tableware in 2013.

Although the local craft, *Takaoka dōki* (Takaoka copperware and bronze casting), is the fruit of a 400-year tradition, today's craftspeople are also interested in keeping up with the times. In addition to bronze casting, there are specialists for tinware and hammered metal products, such as the *orin* gongs. Members of a local association of young craftspeople came up with the idea of creating more products for daily use in order to open up new markets both within and outside Japan. Among other things, the idea for the hammered tin sheets from Syouryu as tableware was developed. With the help of such products, Shimatani Syouryu also want to keep alive the knowledge of traditional hammering techniques, both for their own successors and for Japanese culture.

"Everything we do here only exists because of its everyday use. It's important to respect the traditional techniques and materials and why the form was made a certain way, but we also have to come up with ideas that fit with life in modern society." Kumekazu Shimatani

"To know the correct sound, we have to learn and remember using our whole body, we sort of memorize it through our bodies. It doesn't work like clear notes or like reading a score, it's a very traditional Japanese sound like *shirabe*. *Shirabe* is basically not a clear note, but something like echoes. It's very difficult to describe this in words, but it's like harmonies that echo like 'waowao'. It's very hard to actually get it right. The sound changes by the *shakkan*, the Japanese measurement system. Tuning the echoes and sound is very difficult and requires a high level of practical skill." Kumekazu Shimatani

Structured hammers for working the patterned surfaces of the *suzugami*.

*Suzugami* is available with edge lengths of 11, 13, 18 and 24 cm (4¼, 5, 7 and 9½ in.).

The flexible tin plate can be bent intuitively by hand.

# Shimatani Syouryu Koubou

シマタニ昇龍工房

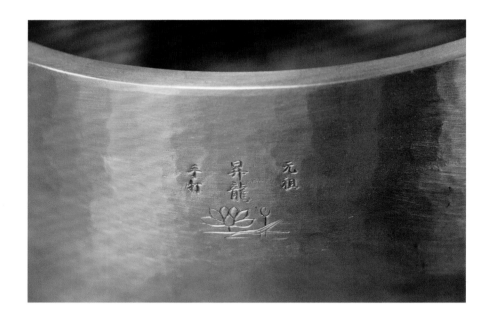

**Shimatani Syouryu Koubou**

# Masami Mizuno

**Metal sheets follow
ideas with hammer blows to
shining perfection**

**Masami Mizuno**

水野　正美

V   VI
VII   VIII

**Masami Mizuno**

Everything seems a little cramped in the two studio rooms that Masami Mizuno set up more than twenty years ago in a former residential building in eastern Nagoya. The passing of time in the rooms is measured in the materials and objects that have gradually accumulated. In the kitchen of the old house, used for brazing and grinding work, the yielding wooden floor almost gives way under a person's steps, while in places the paint is partially peeling. The brown wall plaster and the soft light that falls into the rooms through classic sliding doors and cassette windows bring to mind the warmth of Japanese living spaces. It is the perfect place for Masami Mizuno to hammer his copper and brass goods, which include well-proportioned kettles, pans, pots, plates, spoons, and butter knives on which the word BUTTER is written.

Masami Mizuno appears quite young and relaxed in his modern jeans and casual cardigan, and at the same time completely self-possessed. When you consider that the three-dimensional forms of his works are raised from a flat metal sheet by thousands and thousands of hammer blows, you start to appreciate his artistry.

In traditional *tsuiki* copperware, even the spouts of the classic-looking pots are formed out of the same sheet metal. However, Masami Mizuno sees his pieces as more contemporary, and the details of production are sometimes subordinated to modern design, which does no harm to the aesthetic result.

During hammering he sometimes sits on or in front of a large tree stump, in the top of which special shaping rods are inserted. They are the forming counterpart to the hammers that are used to shape the sheet metal with regular strikes. Quietly murmuring jazz or classical music from the radio weaves in and out of the pattern of hammering where metal meets metal.

Usually, after the copper sheet is cut into a circle, the work is coarsely raised into shape with a wooden hammer, which causes the

An early robot figure shows Masami Mizuno's playful side.

side surfaces to form waves. By hammering in the right places, the volume is deepened, the diameter is reduced and the sides lose their waves. The metal is annealed (heated) part-way through the process to keep it pliable. The diameter is further reduced with the help of various shaping rods and hammers. Additional processing follows after the workpieces have reached their final depth and diameter. Some pots are tin-plated on the inside, some are treated on the outside, but all are planished (polished) with a hammer. Many of these works also receive brass handles that have been hammered and brazed by the artist himself. Finally, Masami Mizuno signs his works on the bottom with his first name in Latin script using a hammer and engraving chisel.

He also spent some time studying the art of screen printing, as can be seen from the drying grids and screens in a small adjoining room. Directly in the entrance area of the house hangs an abstract coloured work by him from 1984.

Some time ago, Masami Mizuno placed a few copper offcuts on two large stones in front of the window. They are now covered with a beautiful oxide patina. The studio itself is home to some of his first metal works, miniature and rather playful in character, including a chair, a park bench and a smiling robot.

水野　正美

I   The former residential house is idyllically tucked away behind high trees.
II   Before being bent, the spout of the drip pot is filled with sand.
III   Two copper teapots with brass fittings.
IV   Masami Mizuno in one of the small studio rooms.

V   With every hammer blow the copper sheet is shaped as well as polished.
VI   The garden contains repurposed remnants of his work.
VII   Copper and brass remains on the table where Masami Mizuno saws and drills.

VIII   Masami Mizuno works on a spout that has just been brazed (joined) to the pot.
IX   Depending on the stage the work is at, he sits on the floor or on the wooden block.
X   An open frying pan and an egg pan.
XI   The drip pot is used to pour the water over the coffee in a manual drip coffee maker.

XII   Pot with openable lid for serving coffee, showing beautiful traces of use.
XIII   Butter knife made of copper and brass, and a small brass spoon.
XIV   The copper and brass objects harmonize well with each other.

A circular copper sheet is cut out for a pot lid.

Smoothing the edge of the lid with a wooden hammer on a wooden block.

A spherical shaping rod helps to shape a brass spoon.

水
野
正
美
**Masami Mizuno** works as an independent copperware craftsman in Nagoya, Aichi Prefecture. He makes every single item by hand, from flat sheet metal to the finished volume.

During his studies, Masami Mizuno would often meet the famous metal artist Takejirō Hasegawa. He began to take an interest in metalworking and was able to learn a great deal, although unfortunately the master did not want to take on an apprentice. However, Masami Mizuno was able to attend some courses at a private school for metalworking under the master's wife, Mami Hasegawa, herself a metal artist. In the famous Gyokusendo workshop in Niigata, he was allowed to spend a few days looking over the shoulders of the masters there. He then taught himself skills in working copper and brass. Because of his own passion for cooking, he mainly produces kitchenware and tableware. The design is entirely by Masami Mizuno himself. He takes his inspiration from fine arts and other things apart from the craft itself.

"When I held my exhibitions, I wanted to exhibit my pot or kettle that I usually use at home. But I cleaned them so that they looked like new ones. Later I realized that an antique look, the beauty of a used one, is very nice, like vintage jeans. So, later, I exhibited my used copperware. Recently, I have intentionally not tried to clean them. When it comes to saucepans, I line the inside with tin. Tin will melt at about 200 °C (392 °F). Tinned copperware changes colour, and the colour of a tinned saucepan will change with heating. Kettles and other utensils, I sometimes intentionally burn them to make their colour like that of a used item. I think it's more beautiful, so for exhibitions I sometimes do that."

Traditional Japanese hammered copper goods are also called *tsuiki dōki*, derived from using a hammer (*tsui*) for the casting (*ki*) of a copper (*dō*) sheet. The actual skill is the so-called raising, the slow and laborious shaping of single flat metal sheets by means of various hammers and shaping rods to form three-dimensional pots, pans or other table and kitchen utensils. Thanks to the compression of the metal during hammering, the pieces must also be repeatedly annealed (softened by heating). Finally, some pieces are also surface-treated for certain purposes.

"I don't make any rough sketches. While I am working, my hand will move automatically and I will just come up with ideas spontaneously. I prefer curved lines. I always have in mind how to express the warmth of copper, which design, which shape is the best for copper."

The heated brass handle of a pot is bent into shape.

Adjusting the handle to the pot.

Adding the maker's signature with hammer and chisel on the bottom of the pot.

**Masami Mizuno**

水野　正美

# Chiyozuru Sadahide Studio

**Old iron still has
another life in the skilful
hands of a blacksmith**

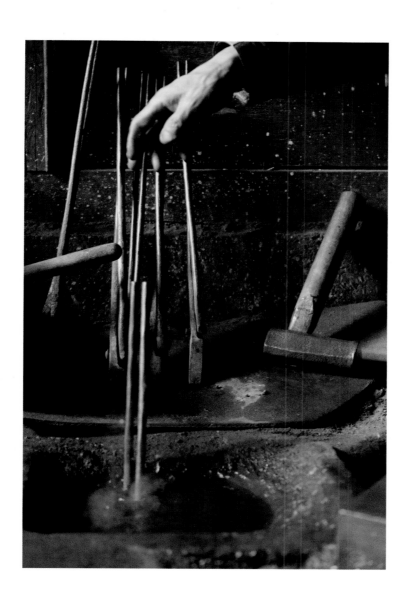

千代鶴貞秀工房

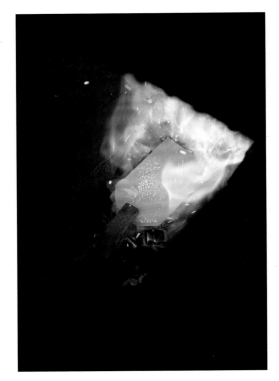

When Iwao Kanki was ready to take over the signature name Chiyozuru Sadahide as a craftsman from his father in the second generation, three conditions were imposed on him. The first was always to remember the honour of bearing this name. The second was always to respect his parents. And the third was to continue learning for the rest of his life.

Chiyozuru Korehide, right, with his son, in front of a Shinto shrine in Tokyo, around 1930.

Chiyozuru Sadahide III, the third generation in the line of bladesmiths, continues this tradition and he is aware of its importance. Naoki Morita – his real name – seems very self-confident in his role, like an ideal successor. Paying tribute to his master, and driven by idealism, conviction and a strong will, he takes on the responsibility of upholding the honour of this craftsman's name with the highest-quality products. According to his guiding principle, the beauty of iron and steel should be inherent in everything he does. Even the new products, such as artistically forged collector's knives or valuable tea-spoons or letter openers, can reveal the raw character of the metal.

When Chiyozuru Sadahide III starts work in his workshop in Ono, he heats up the forge to hammer some blades for Japanese planes from old iron pieces salvaged from a bridge built more than a hundred years ago. A noisy fan blows air through the glowing coals; you can feel the heat and smell the smoky air. An old mechanical forging hammer rushes down, hot sparks splash out. With ear-deafening punches and a few controlled movements, Chiyozuru combines two glowing layers to form the basic shape of a planing knife. A soft iron body forms the backbone, with hard carbon steel for the cutting edge.

Sometimes a bladesmith handles the elements fire, earth, metal, air and water at the same time. Their opposing qualities are noticeable in remarkable physical reactions. The raw forces command total concentration and a healthy respect. The glowing metal, as something true, is the bladesmith's constant self-affirmation at the forge, just as he feels himself through the physical hammer blows with the tensing of every muscle fibre.

Over the next few hours, the metal workpieces are repeatedly made to glow in a forge with a foot-operated bellows. They are shaped and polished by hand with a hammer, files, steel blades, whetstone and grinder. They are relaxed in fine straw ashes, hardened in water and tempered in warm oil. There are numerous process steps, all of them laborious, complicated and physical at the same time.

Perhaps the great self-confidence of artisans also comes from the ability – or the necessity – to control and influence every step taken by hand. Every stroke of a blade-smith, precisely measured and targeted, determines the quality of the blade. Admittedly, tools are usually less about art than about doing something right. No room for interpretation is required. The maker's self-affirmation results from the self-confidence in doing the right thing and, in this case, from the resulting success of the many professional woodworking customers who use his blades.

A knife sharpener perfects Chiyozuru's work by grinding. The result is beautiful, extremely sharp and precise planing knives of a quality that ranks among the best in Japan, perhaps even in the world. No less remarkable are the highly aesthetic craftsperson's knives, also forged from a single piece, which are almost too beautiful to work with.

千代鶴貞秀工房

I   All steps after the rough forging in Ono take place in the workshop in Miki.
II   The glowing blade is hardened in a water bath.
III   Chiyozuru Sadahide II uses a spring hammer to combine the soft iron backing (*jigane*) with the hard carbon-steel cutting layer (*hagane*).
IV   Tools next to the water basin in which a glowing blade is quenched.
V   Anvils are recessed in the ground around the work area where Chiyozuru Sadahide III tests a blade.
VI   The temperature of the metal in the embers can be seen and assessed better in a darkened room.
VII   The forge in the workshop in Miki.

VIII   The temple carpenter Katsumi Yamamoto uses only Chiyozuru Sadahide planing knives.
IX   Chiyozuru Sadahide II and his successor, Chiyozuru Sadahide III.
X   Chip breaker, left, and planing knife with the engraved names Chiyozuru, his former craftsman name Naohide and the master's name Sadahide (right to left).

XI   The craftsman's knife and the spoon for green tea reveal the character of the raw metal.
XII   The softer iron and the hard carbon steel of the cutting edge are clearly visible.
XIII   The finely crafted letter openers are reminiscent of delicate bamboo branches.

Defining the outer shape of the planing knife on the bench grinder.

Flat forging and tempering of the glowing blade.

Removal of unevenness and decoration with a hammer.

二代目 千代鶴貞秀 **Chiyozuru Sadahide II,** born Iwao Kanki, bears this craftsman name in the second generation of the forging line of Chiyozuru, known for their high-quality blades (*kanna*) for Japanese wood planes. He learned bladesmithing from his father, Chiyozuru Sadahide.

三代目 千代鶴貞秀 **Chiyozuru Sadahide III,** born Naoki Morita, was honoured in 2019 to officially continue the name in the third generation, after more than fourteen years of working with his master.

The name Chiyozuru originated with Hiroshi Katō (1874–1957), a great craftsman renowned for forging planing knives during the Shōwa era (1926–1989). His swordsmith ancestors had served the Uesugi samurai clan for centuries. Legend has it that during the ridgepole-raising ceremony of Chiyoda Castle, part of today's imperial palace, a crane flew for three days and nights around the ridge. So Hiroshi Katō gave himself the name Chiyozuru Korehide: "Chiyo" from Chiyoda-jō, and "zuru", derived from the Japanese word for crane (*tsuru*).

"We want to make the people who work with our products proud, because being proud of using these high-quality tools is priceless. [...] Actually, my dream is very simple. I just hope more and more people come to join us and do this work. Because I want to tell them that, even though we now have a lot of great modern factories that manufacture a lot of nice things, manufacturing started here, in workshops like ours. This is the starting point of everything, of making goods. I hope more and more people are interested in that. I don't want to see this traditional work disappear someday in the future. I want so see this keep going on." Chiyozuru Sadahide III

In Japan, high-quality woodworking tools are skilfully forged by hand, mostly by highly specialized craftspeople. The traditional forging techniques for blades were developed in ancient Japan by the *Yamato kaji* (Japanese blacksmiths). The work steps for hand-forged planing knives, scissors, chisels, carving knives and the like are the same. Bladesmiths who want to produce a particularly superlative quality often use iron from late nineteenth-century ship's boilers, railway tracks, anchor chains or dismantled iron bridges, which combine all the required properties in an ideal way.

"When my father went to Tokyo to ask his future master, Chiyozuru Korehide, to teach him, at first he was told: 'If you apprentice with me, you will live your life in poverty like I have. Give up and go home to Banshū.'" Chiyozuru Sadahide II

Close inspection of the concave shape of the plane blade.

Smoothing the metal transition with a two-handled drawknife.

Freehand engraving of the craftsman's name with a hammer and chisel.

# Chiyozuru Sadahide Studio

千代鶴貞秀工房

千代鶴貞秀工房

**Chiyozuru Sadahide Studio**

千代鶴貞秀工房

# Kobayashi Shikki

## In long tradition,
### superimposed, contrasting,
### cautiously renewed

D ust on a freshly painted workpiece would usually be a disaster. But here, seeds or charcoal powder are deliberately trickled onto the moist surface, to be scraped off again after drying. These are the unusual ingredients that, among others, are used in the making of traditional *Tsugaru nuri* lacquer-ware – the northernmost variant of the Japanese *urushi* lacquer craft, which takes its name from the local region, Tsugaru. The finely worked polychrome patterns are applied exclusively by hand. Kobayashi Shikki, a family business from Hirosaki, Aomori Prefecture, is a producer in the sixth generation.

The technique originated around the beginning of the eighteenth century. *Tsugaru nuri* objects developed a very high reputation, serving as status symbols for feudal lords and samurai, who might have a varnished sword scabbard or armour. Today, the variations of this lacquer art adorn countless everyday objects, from tables and boxes to bowls, cups, chopsticks and accessories such as jewelry and even smartphone covers.

The objects to be painted are usually made of wood-based material or specific woods, which the lacquer artists obtain from specialized suppliers. First a special fabric or paper primer is applied to strengthen the thin, light wood. But it is the numerous *urushi* (lacquer)

layers that make it able to withstand the impact of everyday use. The wood's materiality disappears completely under the coating, which makes the products very durable.

*Urushi* hardens through polymerization at suitable temperatures and high humidity. Workpieces are placed in humid drying cabinets for up to twenty-four hours with each new coat of lacquer. Complex samples require up to fifty work steps over as many as ninety days. Lacquer traces can be found throughout the workshop, from the low worktables and the floor to the sliding doors of the drying cabinets and the boards for the freshly lacquered pieces.

The Kobayashi family and employees in front of the store entrance.

There are four major *Tsugaru nuri* styles. *Kara nuri* is a pattern of marbled contrasting colours that is applied with a kind of perforated stencil. Numerous layers of coloured lacquer are then added, dried and sanded down, followed by clear varnishing and polishing. The results are vivid high-contrast patterns in which all applied layers of colour remain partially visible.

*Nanako nuri*, a two-tone pattern evocative of fish roe, is characterized by countless small rings, which are produced by rapeseeds scattered on a damp layer of *urushi*. After they have been scraped off, a contrasting colour is painted over. Everything is sanded, varnished and polished. The pattern is offered in numerous colour combinations.

*Monsha nuri*, made using charcoal powder, has a matt black surface interspersed with glossy details; and *nishiki nuri* is characterized by ornate arabesques or Buddhist patterns applied on a *nanako nuri* background.

Although Kobayashi Shikki have dedicated themselves to the traditional lacquer art, they regularly develop new patterns and product ideas. The family has recognized that even a historic craft so embedded in the Japanese cultural landscape must renew itself in order to appeal to future customers.

小林
漆器

I   Hirosaki lies east of Mount Iwaki, an active volcano.
II   Rapeseeds for the *nanako nuri* pattern are sprinkled on a freshly lacquered serving plate.
III   Detail of a plate in black *nanako nuri* with red highlights.
IV   Hisae Kobayashi at her preferred workplace.

V   Chopsticks are painted in a wide variety of patterns.
VI   Takayuki Kobayashi among the employees' low workstations.
VII   The potter's wheel is generally used to sand round workpieces.

VIII   One of the employees paints a low living-room table.
IX   *Urushi* is mixed directly on the work surface with a triangular spatula (*hera*).
X   Masakazu Kobayashi with *urushi* lacquered pieces in front of the open drying cabinet.

XI   A container and bowl in a unique contemporary interpretation of the *kara nuri* style.
XII   Two-coloured lunch box (*jūbako*) in sepia and grey with contrasting chopsticks.
XIII   Tray, bowl and other tableware with red *nanako* and black *monsha nuri*.

Filtering the *urushi* lacquer by twisting it in fine *washi* paper.

Decorating one of the first layers of the *kara nuri* pattern using a stencil.

Applying the thin lacquer to a bowl with a brush (*hake*).

小林孝幸 **Takayuki Kobayashi,** the fifth generation of the family, joined the Kobayashi Shikki family business straight after high school. They are craft makers of *Tsugaru nuri*, the traditional *urushi* lacquerware of the old castle town of Hirosaki, Aomori Prefecture. He worked in all areas of the business, including sales, before learning the elaborate production of the local lacquerware style from his father.

小林正知 **Masakazu Kobayashi,** the sixth generation, initially worked for a larger company. After an internship within the family workshop he decided to continue the family tradition.

The company was founded around 1830, towards the end of the Edo period (1603–1868), by the ancestors of the Kobayashi family, and is now run by the Kobayashi couple and their son. The family tries to gently refine the traditional styles and to develop new products. They are supported by three employees in the complex painting, sanding and polishing of *Tsugaru nuri* goods.

"Inspiration comes during everyday work, or even when having some sake we might get inspiration for a new pattern or design. [...] *Kara nuri* in *Tsugaru nuri* is especially interesting because there is a lot of variety and you can create more than 10,000 different kinds of coatings." Masakazu Kobayashi

"Depending on the way you use chopsticks, they will last fifteen to twenty years because they go through about thirty steps of coating. My hope is to make such things in the future too. [...] What we have in mind is to make things necessary for our daily life, products that are loved by people and on which you can see the face of the maker."

Takayuki Kobayashi

The plant sap of the lacquer tree (*Toxicodendron vernicifluum*), *urushi* in Japanese, is one of the oldest plant raw materials used by humankind. It is extracted in many East Asian regions and exported to Japan, among other places. A smaller amount is also extracted in certain parts of Japan. During the extraction process, the tree trunks are manually tapped repeatedly over the summer season and the sap collected in several passes by specialized *urushi* harvesters.

In the past, clear *urushi* was mixed with iron oxide and cinnabar for a strong red. Black is traditionally made using soot from organic material. Today, synthetic colour additives are mostly used for an infinite range of colours.

In this craft it has become more and more difficult to find good tools. In particular, the special brushes made from human hair and certain types of animal hair are produced only by very few craftspeople today.

Charcoal powder is sprinkled on the wet paint for *monsha nuri*.

For *nanako nuri* the dried rapeseeds have to be scraped off.

Sanding a bowl with sandpaper and a sponge.

## Kobayashi Shikki

小林
漆器

VII  VIII
IX  X

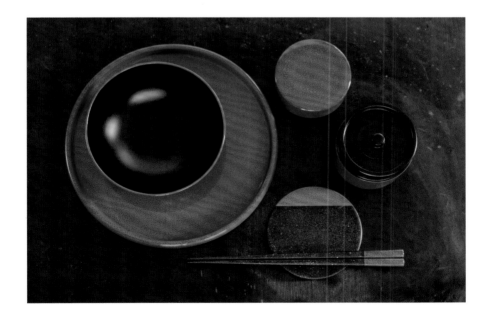

小林漆器

# Junko Yashiro

**Inspired by grain,
ennobled by details of
cumulated depth**

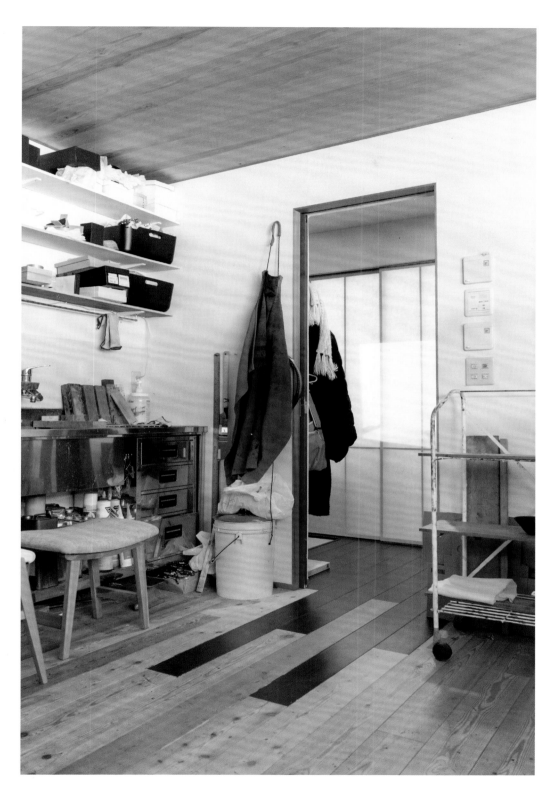

八代　淳子

**Junko Yashiro**

The workshop of an artisan is an unexpected sight in the forests around the elegant highland town of Karuizawa. Yet in the quiet, beautiful place where Junko Yashiro has chosen to settle with her family, vocation and family seem to be ideally compatible in their hideaway.

Junko Yashiro became interested in *urushi* works at an early age, and studied the lacquerware craft at the art university in Tokyo. She liked working with her own hands, but did not initially see herself as an artist. The change came after visiting an exhibition of *urushi* artist Mashiki Masumura. Despite their traditional style, she was impressed by the real-life works that she had previously seen only in books. She was also inspired by Tatsuaki Kuroda, especially by his definition of beauty.

The personality and attitude of another *urushi* artist, Isaburō Kado, were a further source of inspiration. He regarded his pieces as completed only when they were picked up, touched and used. In this vein, Junko Yashiro dedicated herself to the creation of timeless and durable pieces that were equally intended for daily use. Although damaged lacquerware can be repaired if desired, *urushi* lacquered pieces become even more beautiful with prolonged use, especially when wear marks become visible on the surface.

These and similar details of Japanese aesthetics seem to help people in Japan to appreciate the value of craftsmanship again and to want to feel artisans' works with their own hands. This is why lacquerware has become very fashionable again in recent years.

Contrary to the traditional way of working with *urushi*, where the different working stages are separated, Junko Yashiro designs and manufactures the wooden forms, their surfaces, the primer and the finishing completely by herself. She draws her inspiration from magazines and books, from the nature on her doorstep and from the wood itself. When something comes to mind, she immediately makes sketches. Once the idea has matured, she begins with its handcrafted implementation.

The least expected tools for the surface treatment of the pieces

An exciting coincidence of attention to detail is demonstrated around the house by various miniatures of aeroplanes, vehicles and a large shark. Junko's husband, Takeshi Yashiro, a stop motion artist and film director who works in Tokyo, likes to build them out of simple corrugated cardboard with their son at weekends.

are certainly her electric chainsaws. One is used to roughly work out volumes that have not been turned. The sharp teeth of the other chainsaw pull flat, random-looking scores into the surfaces of objects. She works her round rice bowls, sake pots, soy sauce dispensers and containers for matcha tea with a special wood-turning lathe. Other pieces are worked only with knives, chisels and hammers.

The work surface where she does the lacquer work can be identified by its deep black colour, obtained by mixing lacquers with black and various other additives. Spatulas are on the table for this purpose. *Urushi* stands next to it in drums. In Japan, brushes made of human hair are ideally used for application of the lacquer. A sieve made from a bamboo cane helps to apply the preferred tin powder.

Junko Yashiro appreciates the craftsmanship of the traditional lacquer styles, but pursuing her own style has paid off. Her work is characterized by deep black pigments made from pine soot and silvery-warm surfaces. The paper used for reinforcement, like the chainsaw and chisel marks, remains visible. The thinly applied *urushi* and the renewed removal of fresh varnish deliberately make imperfections visible. The result is an unfathomable depth of detail with varying surface textures paired with forms that emanate from her extraordinary sense of proportion.

八代

淳子

A small solid wood bowl is created on the facing lathe.

Rough shaping of a wood bowl with a chisel.

Surface treatment of a tray with a special chainsaw.

八代淳子 **Junko Yashiro** is a talented independent wood and *urushi* artist who lives with her family in Karuizawa, in the east of Nagano Prefecture. She graduated in Urushi Arts, Department of Crafts, from Tokyo University of the Arts.

After her studies, she did not really know what the future would bring. Success came with the consistent implementation of her own ideas. For her modern tableware lines she designs, manufactures and primes all wooden forms herself and then applies the finish using various lacquering techniques. Her work is sold through galleries and individual exhibitions, but she also produces to order, for example for exclusive restaurants.

The caramel-coloured juice of the East Asian lacquer tree (*Toxicodendron vernicifluum*) is called *urushi* in Japan. Its use here can be dated back to the fourth millennium BCE. *Urushi* was originally applied to wooden goods for protection. Over a very long period of time, a unique form of craftsmanship has developed with numerous different styles and techniques across Japan. *Urushi* hardens under warm, humid conditions through polymerization. It remains permanently elastic and resistant to moisture, alcohol, acids and solvents. Its food-safety qualities make it ideal for tableware. It is distinguished by its special shine and depth, qualities that – as with other natural substances – cannot be artificially reproduced.

"I don't have a favourite region or style in Japan for *urushi* lacquerware, because there are so many different perspectives and angles to look at them from. For five or ten years, younger *urushi* artists have gradually been emerging with new creations and I really like that movement. It's good for producing daily tableware, instead of creating museum pieces. [...] A timeless piece can always touch the viewer. So when I started, I decided to devote my life to creating works that are timeless, and that the user can use forever. It wasn't the pieces themselves from those two artists [who influenced me], but this timeless concept behind their work that inspired me and filled me with the idea of being an artist myself."

"I like to include some imperfections in my works, like a crack, a space to breathe, in the otherwise perfectly lacquered surfaces. The colour and texture of tin powder match my works very well because it makes them somehow imperfect."

Thin linen used to reinforce a box is soaked with *urushi*.

A paste made of *urushi* and binding agent levels out any unevenness.

Metal powder is sprinkled onto damp varnish from a sieve tube.

## Junko Yashiro

八代　淳子

**Junko Yashiro**

八代　淳子

# Yanase Washi

**Tender fibre works
of an ancient art, crafted
in synchronous movements**

**Yanase Washi**

やなせ和紙

**Yanase Washi**

It is freezing cold in the large, high hall of the old wooden paper workshop. You can feel the winter here in every bone, though the two craftswomen who scoop sheet after sheet of paper from the large metal vat are seemingly unmoved by the chill.

The omnipresent water is particularly cold here, pure, soft and bubbling in large quantities from the company's own spring. This is something that the original five small communities in the hills of Fukui Prefecture appreciate. Legend has it that in ancient times a princess appeared in the Okamoto River and taught the villagers the art of papermaking. Since then, she has been worshipped as Kawakami Gozen, the deity of paper, and the guardian of paper production for all Japan. Today, the city of Echizen is one of the three most important centres for the production of genuine Japanese paper (*washi*).

The vat for the large *fusuma* paper format, used to cover traditional sliding doors, measures about 3 × 2 m (10 × 6½ ft). A wooden frame with a removable bamboo screen suspended in the middle is operated by a team of two. Before sheets of paper are scooped out, the paper solution, made of prepared plant fibres and the secretion from the roots of the tororo-aoi plant (*neri*, see page 99), is mixed in the vat of water using two old stirring machines and by hand with long sticks. The scooping itself involves each end of the screen being dipped alternately in the liquid multiple

五箇に生まれて紙漉き習うて、横座弁慶で人廻す。

神の授けをそのまま継いで、親も子も漉く孫も漉く。

七つ八つから紙漉き習うて、ネリの合い加減まだ知らぬ。

Echizen traditional papermakers' song:

"Born in Goka and learned papermaking, now managing a paper workshop.

"Passing on the knowledge the deity gave us, parents, children and grandchildren make paper too.

"Having learned papermaking since the age of seven or eight, still don't know enough about mixing *neri* very well."

times, and the screen is oscillated so as to spread the fibres in a homogeneous sheet over its surface.

The next steps are usually dealt with by father and son. They place the pile of dripping wet sheets under solid wooden planks and in a hydraulic press to reduce the water in the layers. The next day they spread the moist sheets on large boards with just a few quick commands between them, in a synchronous choreography. The boards are moved to the drying cabinet, where the sheets lose their remaining moisture. The dried sheets are then cut to size in the paper store under the roof.

A cohesion like that of the Yanase family was a necessity in a craftsperson's family in earlier times. Their good name and entire specialist knowledge were passed on to the next generation so that their children, apprentices or even adopted children could secure their own future. This is still the case today in Japan, especially in the very traditional crafts, and the problem of finding and keeping young talent is all the more serious.

Haruo and Fujiko Yanase therefore seem to be very happy about the initiative of their youngest son to follow them in their own business, not least because they can spend so much time with their offspring. Their daily working life enjoys an informal and familiar atmosphere, which is also transmitted to the employees, who are fairly closely associated with the family.

やなせ和紙

I   A narrow street that leads from the workshop backyard.
II   Tidying up after scooping sheets for the *fusuma* sliding doors (90 × 180 cm / 35 × 70 in.) of traditional Japanese houses.
III   Paper storage and space for cutting and packing.

IV   The Yanase family and staff at the stairs to the paper store.
V   Additional fibres are scooped onto the screen for the *fusuma* sheets.
VI   Fujiko Yanase at the archaic press for the tororo-aoi roots.
VII   Shō Yanase uses a spatula made of bamboo to remove dried paper from the metal sheet.

VIII   Some structured special papers dry in the air.
IX   Numerous rolls of *fusuma* paper in stock.
X   Yanase Washi also creates individual coloured or structural designs.
XI   A *fusuma* sheet and some patterned papers obtained with templates or water effects.

XII   The paper box is additionally varnished with black *urushi*.
XIII   For the "cobble" containers paper fibres are laid over forms.
Design: Ateliers Yoshiki Matsuyama.

Two employees scoop *fusuma* sheets with the large screen.

The sheets are placed on a stack with the bamboo screen.

The paper solution is poured onto the screen for thick or coloured special papers.

柳
瀬
晴
夫
**Haruo Yanase** took over his father's *washi* paper business, Yanase Washi, a long-established family business in one of Japan's most historic paper regions, as a young man. He is an integral member of the papermaking circle of Echizen and the annual festivities for the paper goddess Kawakami Gozen in the local Shinto shrines.

柳
瀬
藤
志
子
**Fujiko Yanase,** Haruo's wife, often coordinates the order processing and works in the creation of smaller paper formats and individual decorative techniques. She plays an active role in a women's cooperative of fifteen local paper companies called Echizen Megami Kurabu (female paper/god club).

柳
瀬
翔
**Shō Yanase,** the youngest of the Yanase family's three sons, is fully involved in the company. He belongs to an independent group of young Echizen papermakers.

For more than 1,500 years, manual papermaking has been a very important craft for the national self-image of the Japanese. *Washi* from Echizen is made from the bark of kōzo (paper mulberry), mitsumata or ganpi shrubs, or hemp. There are different uses and formats. *Hosho* paper is used for woodblock printing (*ukiyo-e*) and certificates, the very fine *gasenshi* for calligraphy, drawings, painting and so on, and the thicker *koma-gami* for labels for sake bottles, postcards, envelopes and the like. In recent years the activity within the guild has intensified so that the papermakers can shape their future together. In this way new ideas for modern design and new applications for paper are taken up.

"For me, after my marriage, I have always felt happy about the craftsmanship. I'm proud of this work. Physically I find it difficult when it's very cold, but I also feel joy when I work. I want to keep the technique, keep the design and everything of *Echizen washi* alive." Fujiko Yanase

"I don't know about the world of *washi*, but I know the current situation of my company. Once I could make *fusuma washi* all day long, there was so much demand, but not so many houses use *fusuma* any more. Currently, people try to combine Western and Japanese design in one house. They have fewer sliding doors – that's why we don't get so many orders for *fusuma washi*. The production is decreasing. So we are trying to invent new products in the meantime. [...] The 100 per cent handmade *washi*, our *fusuma washi*, is also used for the restoration of cultural buildings like temples, shrines and national heritage buildings, and at exclusive Japanese restaurants." Haruo Yanase

Father and son brush sheets on boards for drying in the drying cabinet.

Any protruding fibres are conscientiously removed with small needles.

Dried sheets are pulled off and stacked.

**Yanase Washi**

やなせ和紙

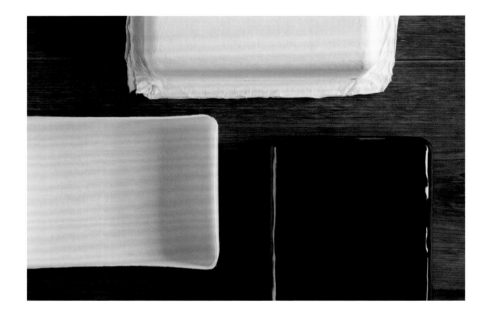

**Yanase Washi**

# Atelier Kawahira

**Fibres in disorder
entwined by skilful movement,
slow ascending steam**

Atelier Kawahira

工房かわひら

In the Hamada region, families traditionally combined two seasonal activities: in the warm months they grew rice and in the winter they made the strong and durable *Sekishū washi* paper, using the particularly long and stable fibres of the kōzo (paper mulberry) shrub. Steep, winding roads lead quickly from the rough and hilly coast into a hidden, deeply incised side valley. Here the Kawahira family live, surrounded by dense forests.

The old work shed crouches next to the main house. A narrow path leads to draughty rooms in which small windows allow little daylight to enter. A spacious workshop with large vats for scooping can be found in the modern wooden building across the street.

The kōzo branches are cut in the fields in December and January before being steamed. The dark outer layer of bark is removed and the inner layer, or bast, is washed and dried.

To dissolve the non-cellulosic materials, the bast must be cooked in an alkaline solution. Among other materials, Atelier Kawahira traditionally uses lime for this purpose. It is an incredibly archaic process that harks back to a different time. An old oil burner hisses under the coarsely built brick fireplace. A cloud of biting steam comes out of the open cooking kettle. Only the edges of things are visible and it is hard to breathe. A white foam

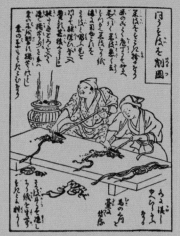

Scraping off the outer part of the kōzo bark. Drawing from Jihei Kunisaki's *Kamisuki Chohoki*, 1798, the oldest manual for paper production in Japan.

swells up in thick bubbles and flows over the pot. In the middle of it all stands Isao Kawahira, holding long wooden sticks with clawlike hooks in his hands. He fishes in the bubbling lava for his kōzo fibres. Only a single weak light bulb illuminates the surreal scene.

Traditionally, the bast is beaten for a long time with an oak stick to loosen the fibres before scooping the paper, but this can also be done by machine in a special beater mill. The roots of the *Abelmoschus manihot* plant, tororo-aoi, are crushed so that they exude a mucilage, known as *neri*. The liquid acts

as a dispersant in the scoop vat and ensures the uniform, homogeneous distribution of the kōzo fibres in the suspension. During repeated scooping, father and son can tell exactly when the right amount of fibres has been distributed evenly on the fine bamboo screen (*suki su*), depending on the intended thickness of the paper sheet. To unroll the wet sheet on the paper pile, the screen is removed from the hinoki wood frame (*suki keta*). The *neri* also allows the individual sheets to remain separate, so they can be placed on top of each other. A spindle press squeezes the excess water out of the completed stack. The following day, the sheets are dried on heated metal surfaces or in the sun attached to wooden boards.

The family are aware of their special way of life as rice farmers and papermakers. They want to keep the economic balance and at the same time remain independent. It is important for them to keep alive the traditional knowledge and techniques. The father, Masao Kawahira, passed on the know-how not only to his son, but also to the people of Bhutan in his younger years. The trend in craftsmanship to devote oneself to raw materials, processing and finished product was already evident in his work decades ago. And Isao Kawahira, his son, also innovates in his arts and crafts through cooperations with designers.

工房かわひら

I The dense forest behind the house is inhabited by wild boar.
II Paper sheets are made by scooping the solution onto the bamboo screen.
III Metal surfaces heated with a fire quickly dry the damp sheets.
IV Freshly cut kōzo branches wait for the first steaming.

V Masao Kawahira stands next to the new workshop in a traditionally cut jacket woven entirely from paper yarn.
VI The old workshop is right next to the Kawahira family house.
VII The paper workshop with the press (left) and the ladling vat (right).
VIII Before being cooked in lime lye, the bast is washed.

IX Isao Kawahira next to the old workshop, with the kōzo boiling inside.
X A roll with forty sheets of *Sekishū-banshi* paper on some kōzo branches.
XI The thinness of the paper can be seen by the lowness of this stack of 200 sheets.
XII Parents can sew these paper baby slippers from a kit.

XIII Paper yarns can be spun from dyed paper fibres.
XIV Sheets that have not yet been cut still have the frayed, or deckle, edges from the scooping.

Freshly cut and bundled kōzo twigs.

Scraping the bast with a knife.

The old-style cooking of the soaked bast in a lime lye.

川平正男 **Masao Kawahira** runs the Kawahira family business from the town of Misumi, Shimane Prefecture. The family grow rice in summer, and make *Sekishū washi* paper from the fibres of kōzo shrubs in winter. He originally worked in a shipyard near Hiroshima, but then began to make paper at his parents' workshop. He has spent time in Bhutan as a papermaking teacher and is chairman of the Sekishū-banshi Craftsmen's Association.

川平勇雄 **Isao Kawahira** worked as an auctioneer at the famous Tsukiji Fish Market in Tokyo. He came back to Misumi to take up the family tradition and continues it with a great sense of mission.

Atelier Kawahira produce calligraphy paper, sheets for certificates, papers with watermarks and postcards. In addition, they supply special *washi* paper to craftspeople who produce common leaf fans (*uchiwa*) and folding fans (*sensu*). They have worked with a designer to develop baby slippers made of paper, and they spin paper yarn from kōzo fibres. Today the family

"My father is my master, but sometimes I have a chance to look at the work from other workshops and I can learn a lot from them. Basically, making mistakes is very important. They make me develop. My father allows me to make mistakes. I'm grateful for this. When I make paper I do it with great concentration. I make very high demands of myself. I have not been taught by my father to 'do this' or 'don't do it like this'. I learned the basic techniques. I think it is important to acquire techniques for myself. I'm on the way. I will have finished when I die. Until then I will always have a sense of challenge." Isao Kawahira

business is one of only four papermakers in Misumi, where formerly there were hundreds.

The *Sekishū washi* from the region (previously called Sekishū or Iwami, today part of Shimane Prefecture) has been produced for more than 1,300 years with techniques that are almost unchanged. Fibres from cultivated kōzo (paper mulberry) and mitsumata (*Edgeworthia chrysantha*) as well as the wild-growing ganpi (*Wikstroemia*) are used. The paper is also called *Sekishū-banshi* ("half sheets of Sekishū") because of its format. It has been placed on UNESCO's Representative List of the Intangible Cultural Heritage of Humanity.

"I worked in Hiroshima for about ten years, and I saw a different world, unrelated to making paper. A child needs to go away from the family and encounter difficulties, but also learn a lot." Masao Kawahira

All impurities from the fibres are removed in a water bath.

Kōzo fibres and *neri* are mixed in the vat using a rake.

The still moist sheets are brushed onto wooden boards to dry in the sun.

# Atelier Kawahira

工房かわひら

**Atelier Kawahira**

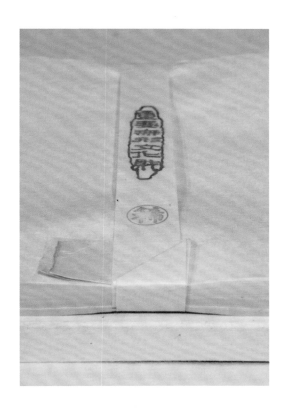

工房かわひら

XI XII
XIII XIV

# Take Kobo Once

**Braided elegance
blossoms beautifully in
idyllic remoteness**

**Take Kobo Once**

竹工房オンセ

**Take Kobo Once**

Luckily, there is no snow yet on the steep, narrow roads to the studio of Masato Takae. Two log buildings are located idyllically among woods, meadows and terraced fields. Built from massive tree trunks, they look as though they have been transported from another world to the mountains above Beppu. In this remote area, the artisan and his employees make exquisite bamboo basketry.

Traditionally, the utensils required for the Japanese tea ceremony were often kept in small plaited bamboo baskets (*chakago*) to protect them, although over the years demand for them has decreased. Masato Takae was inspired by these accessories to create the finely woven handbags that are his most elaborate, valuable and successful products.

When he took up the profession more than thirty years ago, the entire production process appealed to him – the transformation of tall, thin, straight plants without great intrinsic value into three-dimensional forms of great beauty, woven in geometric patterns. His bags range from small handbags to big shoppers to stylish baskets, natural or coloured, whether elegant black, extroverted red or distinguished dark brown with a waxed surface.

The bamboo culms are transformed into thin, flexible strips by repeatedly splitting and reducing width and thickness. Strip-making accounts for 50 per cent of the total work on a bag. After peeling

Masato Takae relied on the helping hands of his cheerful friends and colleagues for the lengthy construction of his wooden log house from 1985 onwards.

the outer skin and cutting to the required length, Masato Takae splits the bamboo culm with a massive bamboo cutting knife or a radial splitting knife. Next he pulls the bamboo strips through two extremely sharp, pointed tool blades to break the edges and define the exact width. He reduces the thickness of the strips and planes the nodes using a device with a horizontal blade. All the tools he uses are amazingly simple and efficient.

The result is a bundle of identical strips, in some cases already dyed. He starts the complex weaving process at the bottom of the bag or basket. It is always based on

pre-calculated patterns. As soon as the surface is large enough, it is permanently bent upwards with moisture and heat. The corners are plaited and reinforced and the upper edge skilfully bordered. Masato Takae's bags only have plaited joints, which makes them repairable, and thanks to the unique natural material and the *urushi* finish they are surprisingly durable.

The handbags also incorporate other traditional Japanese crafts. The lavish woven fabrics of the inner bags, for example, come from Amami Ōshima, an island northeast of Okinawa where traditional weaving and mud dyeing are still practised. The cords for closing the bags are woven by craftspeople from Mie Prefecture using the old *Iga kumihimo* technique.

Masato Takae has a flair for sales, and is communicative, fearless and resolutely optimistic. He knows the value of a brand name, fed by constant high quality, design and handcrafted finesse. His handbags and shoppers, although of a different nature, can compete with European luxury brands. His flower baskets are works of art that complement and enhance flower arrangements.

The two houses in the woods were built by himself and his wife, with the help of friends. Today, there is no end-of-year *mochi-tsuki* (tradition of rice pounding to make *mochi*, or rice cakes) or pizza-baking in his home-built stone pizza oven without inviting friends and associates.

竹工房オンセ

The outer skin of the bamboo culm is removed with a curved knife.

Marking the places where the bamboo culm is to be split.

Rough removal of the knots with a special knife.

高
江
雅
人
**Masato Takae** founded his studio for bamboo basketry, Take Kobo Once, in 1993 in the mountainous backcountry of Beppu, a town on Kyūshū island famous for its thermal springs.

While travelling across Japan as a young man, Masato Takae became interested in cooking. After attending a cookery school, he found a job in an early organic restaurant. After a while he devoted himself to organic farming, but had to find a supplementary income. He then discovered the vocational school for *Beppu take zaiku* (bamboo basketry from Beppu), which was the starting point for his successful career as a craftsman there. Owing to its remote southern location, he spends about a third of the year travelling, promoting his products in Japan's luxury department stores.

The making of traditional bamboo basketry from Beppu has always afforded a secondary income to local farmers. Since the Beppu occupational school was founded around 1903, its talented graduates have shaped the renowned bamboo craft from Beppu, internationally as well as at home. All students spend two years studying, following which they usually look for an apprenticeship with an established craftsperson for a further three to five years.

In Masato Takae's craft workshop, the young craftspeople learn all the processes, from the beginning to the finished product. After a while they are allowed to make products themselves. He even supports them after the apprenticeship in order to simplify their start in the craft. Up to twelve employees work in his studio in sales and production.

"I would say my life is quite fortunate. People around me always say I have a hard time doing this job, but I never think of it like this. The situation is always changing, and in the future it might change again. So I have to change myself to fit."

"The *hitori* process, the strip-making, is the most time-consuming part of the process, but it will decide the quality of the product. Fifty per cent is decided by the quality of the strips. If you make good strips, you can easily make good weaving. [...] Tools are very simple, for example I break the corners of the strips just using two blades. Of course there are machines, but when you use these simple tools, even a craftsman with one simple tool can work by himself. The characteristics of each bamboo are different and machines cannot be easily adjusted, so nobody thinks to depend on expensive machinery."

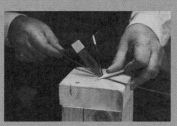
Exact width is achieved by pulling strips between two special blades.

The weaving of the bag structure starts at the centre of the base.

Bag edges are knotted with thin rattan strips.

**Take Kobo Once**

竹工房オンセ

X     **Take Kobo Once**

竹工房オンセ

XI  XII
XIII  XIV

# Hajime Nakatomi

## Artistic freedom, thought-out and calculated, fortunate numbers

# Hajime Nakatomi

中臣 一

The radio plays jazz classics. Light pours through large windows into the white room with its walls of perforated panels. The floor consists of three stepped terraces. Below the windows stand identical tables, with the same office chairs, lights and heating elements. Thick bamboo canes are stored behind a large window in a small room that looks like a recording studio. On the opposite wall hangs a large lined whiteboard with handwritten notes. A few tools hang tidily on hooks in an open cabinet. Structures resembling small metal fir trees stand to one side, tapered at the top, rotationally symmetrical, with serrated edges.

This is the former music room of an old comprehensive school, and the present studio of Hajime Nakatomi. Here the artist, who exhibits his works internationally, creates fascinating objects out of bamboo, influenced by mathematics, geometry and symmetry.

Decades ago Shōunsai Shōno and other artisans created exquisite objects from bamboo and rattan with nothing but bamboo strips, simple tools and their own hands. Today they look like complex computer models. Twenty years ago, the impression these works made on Hajime Nakatomi was so profound that he felt the desire to create something like them himself.

He approaches his complex pieces somewhat like an engineer.

"Infinite Shadow" bamboo chandelier, 240 cm (94½ in.) (h) × 164 cm (64½ in.) (diam.), realized by Hajime Nakatomi, Yasumichi Morita and Hidetoshi Nakata.

The calculation of parameters is the basis of his work and passion at the same time. In his world of numbers he finds the beauty of geometry and symmetry, the elegance of simple circles, triangles, squares, ellipses and figure-eights. Repeated many times, pure geometry can also take on organic forms, comparable to a macroscopic view of microscopic structures inherent in nature.

Mysteriously intertwined objects, weightless and repetitive, are lined up on two tables. A twisted, complicated-looking flower vase has been tied from up to 1,000 knots and bows. Its compact form is misleading, however: it is light as

a feather. In other works, triangles made of three combined eights form complex shapes. His "Prism" series consists of multiple linear pyramids, each pyramid made of two triangles, that form flexible structures. All connections are plaited and knotted, if necessary with tweezers. *Urushi* in shades of red or black makes the natural material durable. There are no standardardized objects here: they are individual works of art.

Hajime Nakatomi appreciates the routine of frequently repeated steps in his work, such as tying the numerous small knots that hold the bamboo strips together. The extraordinary, elaborate chandeliers made of bamboo strips are one of his specialities, for whose construction he uses the peculiar metal trees as scaffolding. He also likes to create more classic bamboo objects, such as the hexagonal platter of loops for the presentation of traditional *wagashi* sweets during the tea ceremony.

Hajime Nakatomi's ideal balance would be 50 per cent commissioned work and 50 per cent personal creation. He would fill any spare time with experiments and small studies, like the ones that can be found in the studio today. Maybe one day he will realize his vision of having his works and those of other Japanese bamboo artists tour in a series of exhibitions – worldwide, in many places, like a "rock band" of bamboo art, as he himself puts it.

中臣一

I   An artist from the TSG project (see page 282) stands in the bamboo grove near Taketa Castle.
II   Hajime Nakatomi prepares one of his basic elements from three connected bamboo eights. In Japan, eight is a lucky number, and his works can be read as wishes for continual happiness.

III   The artist and a young colleague from the TSG project making bamboo strips.
IV–XI   Small samples; details; two objects based on triangles from his "Prism" series; a plaited *wagashi* coaster; and an object based on "eight"-elements.

XII   Hajime Nakatomi stands in front of the whiteboard on a floor working area.
XIII   Small balls braided from bamboo strips and coloured red are coated with clear *urushi*.
XIV   In the former recording studio bamboo culms of different diameters are stored.

XV   A tall, light object made of dozens of coloured basic "eight"-elements.
XVI   The elaborate flower vase consists of up to 1,000 knots; each red string comprises six very thin bamboo strips.

Rough stripping the outer skin of a madake bamboo culm.

To obtain the harder layer, strips are split in thickness.

The required thickness is finally achieved by a special device with a horizontal blade.

中
臣
一 Hajime Nakatomi studied business marketing at Waseda University in Tokyo, but he was profoundly impressed by the work of Living National Treasure Shōunsai Shōno (1904–1974) and other bamboo artists. Instead of going into marketing, he followed his heart and trained at the Ōita Prefectural Bamboo Crafts Training Center and on a further specialist training course.

The renowned bamboo artist Syōryū Honda took him on as an apprentice for three more years. In the last year of his apprenticeship he was able to work on his own pieces, and in 2005 felt confident enough to open his own studio.

Hajime Nakatomi produces art objects for interior design, such as chandeliers or high-quality bamboo wall coverings as part of larger commissions, and he creates smaller objects for exhibitions in Japan, North and South America and Asia.

Long ago, simple containers for storing food were woven from bamboo strips. Over time, different techniques for higher-value objects

developed. Elaborate containers for the storage of valuable bowls for the Japanese tea ceremony or vases for the Japanese art of flower arranging marked a highlight in the artistry of this highly developed craft, which has been surpassed by the development of pure art objects since the 1950s.

Exhibitions of bamboo objects are one of the few opportunities for young artists to sell their work. In Taketa artisans support each other in a kind of network. Hajime Nakatomi sometimes supports younger colleagues by asking them to take over the important basic strip-making for him.

"Having control of the material as well is quite rare in Japan. When you think of ten or twenty years in the future, I'm quite sure that you will not be able to get high-quality bamboo. I think this is a turning point for bamboo art."

"I like moving my hands in doing a job such as making knots very much. When people see it, they may think 'oh, it is a boring job', but for me, bamboo strings differ from one piece to another. I feel differences because I do routine work, routine jobs. If everything were dramatic, I might not feel the differences. Routine work means much to me and I believe it's actually good for people – otherwise you just cannot keep working on bamboo. […] I really like numbers, I really like mathematics. And bamboo craft requires calculation of structural strength. Bamboo art in my view is a world of numbers. And I feel it is very much natural to me, it really fits my character."

For cutting, mature bamboo culms with a sufficient density of growth are selected.

The connection detail of a basic element measures only about 5 × 5 mm (¼ × ¼ in.).

The artist paints a bamboo object with dark *urushi* to protect the surface.

# Hajime Nakatomi

中臣一

**Hajime Nakatomi**

**Hajime Nakatomi**

中臣一

# BUAISOU

**The whole year round
some friends and indigo plants
together, they grow**

There were two of them at first. But soon friends with more contacts and experience came along, and BUAISOU were able to position themselves across a broader range. In contrast to the traditional mode of craft specialization in Japan, they focus on a holistic business model by offering own-grown and own-processed indigo and dyeing from a single source.

They work in synchrony with the planting cycle and the seasons. The field shall be ploughed, the indigo seeds sown and the seedlings planted. The plants must be watered and harvested and the valuable leaves separated from the stems and dried.

Everything is done with the aim of creating the basis for dyeing: the fermented, dried and preserved indigo leaves known as *sukumo*. This natural dye produces a unique deep blue colour, or lighter shades if desired. The fermentation process of the leaves is called *nekasu* ("letting sleep"), which takes place in a special room, the *nedoko* ("sleeping room") over about four months in winter. This organic material is turned and aired once a week, an arduous process during which the steaming air saturated with ammonia makes it hard to breathe.

BUAISOU use the *sukumo* in a heated lye of wood ash from

One of BUAISOU's greenhouses serving multiple purposes throughout the year.

smoking *katsuobushi* (bonito flakes), shell lime and wheat bran as a nutrient. This challenging traditional method based on a fermentation process in the vat is called *jigoku date* (literally, "producing hell") and it makes the indigo dye pigment soluble. The initially colourless indigo reacts in the presence of atmospheric oxygen, turning from yellow-green to blue on the dyed material. Indigo from Tokushima is also called *Awa ai*, Awa being the old name of the region. *Ai* means indigo-dyed blue, but it also means love. Beloved blue. You have to love it to give it this much care and attention.

Throughout the year, BUAISOU dye the textiles or other things their customers ask for, and, if required, produce screen-printing templates for them. Last but not least, they design and sew a range of their own products. With the realization of BUAISOU jeans one of their dreams as indigo dyers has come true. They

even dye the yarn used for weaving the denim.

For their attitude they are highly appreciated in the younger Japanese craft scene. The conceptual approach turns them into a new species of craftsperson. Young, willing to take risks, creative, interdisciplinary, and at the same time locally analogue and digitally networked worldwide. Craftspeople are often considered to have little affinity for the digital world, digital devices being largely useless for physical work with one's own hands. But BUAISOU could be described as a handicraft influencer, with Instagram as their digital tool. The platform ensures a constant flow of interested fans and customers.

A remarkable crowd of fans on social media follows the worldwide travels of the craftworkers and their cyclical activities in the fields. The followers enjoy seeing the results of participants in the dyeing courses run by BUAISOU in Tokushima and abroad, when they get invited by companies and organizations; collaborations with other brands; and of course BUAISOU's own indigo-dyed products. Thanks to high-quality photographs, the young collective elegantly present the aesthetics of painstaking work. They also show the appeal that a simple, seemingly more old-fashioned life can have. It is their philosophy.

B
U
A
I
S
O
U

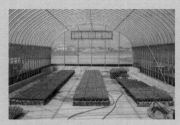

Young indigo plants are grown in greenhouses.

Planting seedlings, watering and weeding in the field.

*Kirikaeshi*, the weekly watering and stirring of the fermenting leaves.

楮
覚
郎
**Kakuo Kaji** became interested in natural dyeing with indigo during his studies in textile design. He co-founded the brand BUAISOU with a craftsman he met at a local programme to encourage young farmers and indigo dyers back to the traditional indigo region of Tokushima.

結
城
研
**Ken Yuki** studied the fermentation of indigo under highly acclaimed *sukumo* master Osamu Nii. The process was originally developed in Awa province (today part of Tokushima Prefecture) around the sixteenth century.

三
浦
佑
也
**Yuya Miura** was involved in the design and manufacture of indigo-dyed textiles before he joined BUAISOU.

Besides these three, Tadashi Kozono joined the team after a few years, while Kyoko Nishimoto has been responsible for public relations and social media for a long time.
    Today's producers of *sukumo* are dependent on buying the indigo plant (*Polygonum tinctorium*) from local farmers or growing it

"Some people say Tokushima is the centre of indigo dyeing, but it's more the centre of *sukumo*. The center of indigo dyeing is Kyoto or other places here in Japan. [...] Actually, there are only five *sukumo* makers in Tokushima right now, and two more in other regions. At BUAISOU we make *sukumo* and at the same time we do indigo dyeing. A long time ago there were famous indigo-dyeing teachers from Kyoto and Fukuoka. We have only been doing this for a few years, but we feel each place, each dyer, is different. The last time, a famous indigo-dyeing teacher came from Miyazaki. I felt that the indigo-dyeing process from there is totally different from ours." Kakuo Kaji

themselves. Custom dyers only dye clothes, fabrics, yarns and sometimes small accessories made of natural materials such as wood or leather. Indigo dyers also often offer workshops in which you can dye your own garment, bag or shawl with a screen print or batik motif you have created yourself. And then there is BUAISOU, who offer everything from a single source: growing indigo plants, *sukumo* making, dyeing textiles and unusual objects, workshops, sewing and fashion from their own production.

"My dream is just to go on and do indigo dyeing continually, and not give up. Even if our staff were more than 100 people, like in a big company, I would want to continue farming, dyeing, sewing, designing by myself. And even if this company were only one person, I would like to do the same. That's all." Kakuo Kaji

The *sukumo* is raked into a neat pile after it has finished airing.

The dye solution is mixed from the dried *sukumo* and other ingredients.

Dyeing takes place all year round in heated dyeing vats.

**BUAISOU**

BUAISOU

**BUAISOU**

VI VII
VIII IX

# ISSO

**Skilful refinement,
little becomes opulent,
what a noble art**

The exciting architecture of Tokiko Kajimoto's house was specially designed to meet her needs. An octagonal tower at the end of the building houses her studio, where three clay vats for traditional indigo dyeing are sunk into the ground. A massive trunk supports the wooden structure of the octagonal dyeing room. The walls between the corner trunks are made of natural materials. A wooden staircase winds up to the second and third levels, where the floors are made of bamboo canes, a simple construction that allows air to circulate. When the shutters near the ground are open, the vapours from the dye bath can rise freely, escaping via the roof opening. At the same time, the exposed concrete in the narrow horizontal living area reflects a modern understanding of architecture in Japan.

Tokiko Kajimoto always had a special interest in ceramics and other handicrafts used in daily life. One day she saw works by the famous dyer Motohiko Katano and was deeply impressed by them. She made the decision to go to Tokushima, her husband's hometown, to learn the dyeing craft there. The roots of Japanese *sukumo* craftsmanship lie in the former Awa region, today's Tokushima Prefecture. There she found in Toshiharu Furushō an excellent teacher who taught her the secrets of indigo dyeing based on *sukumo*. It was the foundation of her own existence as an artisan.

Like every dyer, Tokiko Kajimoto has a special relationship with her dye. In the Furushō dye shop, she worked with the *sukumo* of Osamu Nii from Tokushima. Even today she trusts in the master's fermented indigo leaves. The ash for the lye

The inserted floors in the studio are made of bamboo canes. The outside staircase of the house is a timber construction.

comes from the stone oven of a pizza bakery. And to the bacteria in the fermenting dye solution, she adds a good dash of Tokushima-brewed sake as a nutrient.

In dyeing itself, she is interested in the results of dyeing fabrics with different yarns, origins and tactility. She particularly likes colour gradients, which are difficult to create in dyeing. The uniform colouring of a transition, from white or undyed to deep blue, must always be matched

to the type of fabric and requires a great deal of experience.

Products from ISSO include the tender-looking, airy, almost transparent silk scarves woven in Kiryū, Gunma Prefecture. Their long, narrow shape is perfect for beautiful colour gradients. But there is also a blue split curtain with charming white polka dots. Soft fringed scarves of Indian cotton are dyed in deep blue. A narrow table runner consists of coarse hemp fibres; several of them with colour gradients become an attractive tapestry when placed side by side.

Another speciality of Tokiko Kajimoto is large tapestries dyed in graphic patterns. Using the complex and precise shaped-resist technique *itajime shibori*, she can also realize small colour transitions with high contrasts. Especially tricky are additional uncoloured or deep blue lines. In this way she gives the fabrics a strong graphic feel, as in the artistic commissions for interiors in upscale hotels or Japanese holiday resorts. The varying contrast of different-coloured areas elegantly reveals the craftsmanship value of an artwork.

This is the traditional symbiotic working method of Japanese indigo dyers – refining the high-quality products manufactured by other artisans. Tokiko Kajimoto's art is in the knowledge of the organic nature of indigo and the control over the dynamics of dyeing, which she applies to her own pieces in a masterly way.

一
草

I   The three-storey house with studio.
II   Tokiko Kajimoto inspects the result of a silk scarf just dyed with a gradient.
III   Gradient-coloured lampshade in the entrance area of the house.

IV   Dyeing of silk scarves in indigo gradients by the successive unwinding of a stick.
V   A dyeing vat of glazed ceramic embedded in the floor, with one of the ventilation hatches open in the background.

VI   Two scarves hang from a bar to dry after dyeing.
VII   Tokiko Kajimoto in the dining area of her house. One of her indigo mobiles hangs to the side.
VIII   One of her tapestries hangs as an object in the dyeing studio.

IX   During the dyeing process, every detail was controlled by elaborate folding and tying.

Crushing the *sukumo* lumps before preparing the dye solution.

Sake is added as a nutrient for the bacteria.

Before dyeing, the indigo "flower" formed by the bacteria is skimmed off.

梶
本
登
基
子

**Tokiko Kajimoto** is an indigo-dyeing artist from Tokushima, Tokushima Prefecture, who learned her craft from a well-known local dyer. She and her son, Yudai Kajimoto, produce and sell their own products under the name ISSO.

ISSO also do commissioned work, such as dyeing large tapestries, and collaborate on dyeing projects. Her motivation is to convey the beauty of indigo (*ai*) at all times. She likes to use resist-dyeing techniques (*shibori*) – partial dyeing through the binding of fabrics to create a pattern. She enjoys exploring a great variety of fabrics to develop new products, dye patterns or complete artworks. Her works are offered by boutiques as well as shown in galleries and exhibitions. ISSO are also represented regularly at European lifestyle fairs such as Maison & Objet in Paris with their silk scarves and other products.

    Dyeing with pigments from minerals, plants or animals is one of the oldest cultural techniques.

Knowledge handed down was often lost over time, particularly since the invention of synthetic colours in the nineteenth century. Nonetheless, dyeing with indigo has remained a living part of the culture in Japan, while textiles dyed in a natural way are enjoying increasing popularity worldwide. Every indigo dyer who works with traditional methods wants to keep the basis for natural dyeing alive and to produce excellent products. Their buyers are also willing to accept higher prices, in support of elaborate and genuine craftsmanship.

"I sometimes go looking for potential fabrics for my works, or sometimes I happen to 'meet' them by chance. I study the material and make a design that is suitable for it. I turn it into an artwork or a product. What's most important to me is that the design supports and brings out the beauty of *ai*."

"The current situation of indigo in Tokushima is that there are far too few *aishi san* [indigo masters] who make *sukumo*, four or five people only. I feel a little anxious about the situation, but a next generation is growing, so I am looking towards the future without too much of a worry. Also, people who use indigo are increasing again. There are more opportunities to introduce indigo; young people are interested and some of them have started new businesses. I feel hope there. All over Japan there are people making a living out of indigo dyeing."

Undyed fabrics are folded on a shelf.

When dyeing with indigo, the dyer's hands also take on the blue colour.

Each hand-dyed piece is unique.

**ISSO**

一草

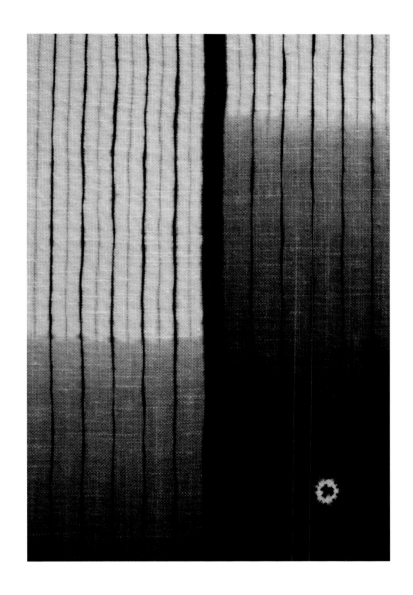

草

一

# Tree to Green

Long grown on hillsides,
follows on the valley ground
their transformation

**Tree to Green**

The river is blanketed in fog. Clouds hang deep in the valley and cover the densely forested hills. Shreds of clouds gather from side valleys, while water rushes everywhere. Hinoki, sawara, kōyamaki, nezuko and hiba trees are arrayed in infinite gradations of dark green. These are the "five sacred trees" of Kiso. This seems the most mystical place in Japan.

The tortuous valley in Nagano and Gifu Prefecture, through which the Kiso River flows, has a felicitous population of trees. Hinoki cypress in particular is highly valued in Japan for its water resistance, scent and essential oils. Among other things, it is one of the preferred woods for building Buddhist temples and Shinto shrines. The highest honour is given to the hinoki tree by its use in the Ise Jingū (Ise Grand Shrine) in Mie Prefecture, which is ritually rebuilt every twenty years. The most important Shinto shrine in Japan, the Grand Shrine is visited by six million pilgrims every year.

Tree to Green want to strengthen the forestry industry in Japan with modern products and business services. They also want to contribute to the preservation of Japanese crafts. With nearly 70 per cent of its land covered by woods, Japan is one of the most forested countries in the world. Yet up to 70 per cent of the wood it uses is imported, as

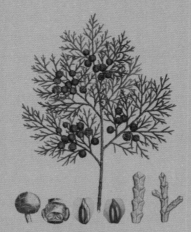

Hinoki cypress. Drawing by Philipp Franz von Siebold and Joseph Gerhard Zuccarini, *Flora Japonica*, 1835–70.

other countries harvest larger quantities at lower cost.

Besides the quality timber, there are also highly qualified craftsmen and numerous wood-processing companies in the Kiso Valley. Tree to Green run their own workshop in an old-established former joinery. Previously, about thirty craftsmen worked here building altars for Shinto shrines and miniature household altars. Fortunately, the new impulses from Yusuke Aono and co-founder Takanori Kosegi have preserved the location and the know-how. The connection to the Kiso Valley proved a stroke of luck.

Takanori Kosegi was born and raised in the Kiso Valley. His grandfather founded Kosegi Mokko (Kosegi Woodwork), which is now

run by his parents. The family business also manufactures products for Tree to Green and is located a few kilometres further south in the valley. This is another place to encounter the atmosphere of past decades, with its wonderful soft light, old machinery, floors marked with use, and piles of wood dust.

Tree to Green also cooperates with other local craft businesses: Okekazu manufactures oke (barrel) products, Yamaichi Ogura Rokuro Crafts turns a series of bowls and TATEMOKU produces furniture for individual interior projects.

The founders of Tree to Green and the sub-brand Kiso Lifestyle Labo had the vision to develop, manufacture and market their own contemporary products from Japanese wood. They have a timeless, modern style and range from bath products to kitchen utensils typical of Kiso. Parallel to this, they have developed a successful business planning and producing interiors for nursery schools, for example, also made of local wood.

In Tokyo, a team of about twenty people from all parts of Japan, including directors for the different business sections, designers, constructors and office staff, joined Yusuke Aono and Takanori Kosegi within six years. And the company is still growing, thanks to its smart concepts and new visions for an enduring relationship between the Japanese and their woods.

I   The rushing river Atera flows from a narrow side valley into the Kiso.
II   Finishing Kiso Lifestyle Labo bath stools for use in Japanese *onsen* (hot springs).
III   Tree to Green work almost entirely with wood from the local Kiso region.
IV   Jungo Suzuki (left), Mr Hara (right), and another staff member in the production department.

V   A retired carpenter, Mr Hara supports the team with his expertise.
VI   A stationary router in the buildings of the large joinery.
VII   Takanori Kosegi, one of the two founders, in his parents' workshop.
VIII   Some finished bath stools of the sub-brand Kiso Lifestyle Labo, made of water-resistant hinoki wood.

IX   With the big bandsaw Hideo Kosegi can also deliver long boards.
X   The workshop and sawmill of Kosegi Mokko in the Kiso Valley.
XI   Hideo Kosegi and his wife in their workshop.
XII   Kosegi Mokko manufactures for Tree to Green, among others.
XIII   The interior of Kosegi Mokko's long workshop building near Nojiri.

XIV–XVIII   Products from Kiso Lifestyle Labo: water-resistant hinoki bath mat with silicone feet; aromatic hanger made of fragrant hinoki; water-resistant hinoki bath stool; aromatic hinoki bath flakes in a water-permeable bag*; water-resistant hinoki soap dish*.

* photographs by Tree to Green

The oval trademark of Kiso Lifestyle Labo is burned into a stool.

Two of the woodworkers discuss production steps in the workshop.

Beautiful daylight atmosphere in Tree to Green's temporary workshop building.

青野裕介 **Yusuke Aono** is president of Tree to Green, a company from Tokyo committed to a more sustainable use of Japanese wood resources. Trained as a lawyer, he worked in the banking, consulting and energy sectors before co-founding Tree to Green in 2013. The company offers lifestyle products and interiors made of wood as well as workshops and business consulting in a wide range of fields, including support for childcare facilities.

小瀬木隆典 **Takanori Kosegi** is co-founder of Tree to Green and director of products and woodworking workshops. He grew up in the Kiso Valley and rediscovered his connection to the nature of this important woodworking region during his studies in Tokyo.

小瀬木日出男 **Hideo Kosegi**, Takanori's father, has worked in the wood industry for many years and has been a director of Tree to Green since 2015. He also continues to run the Kosegi Mokko family business in the lower Kiso Valley.

"The huge Kiso Valley is full of hinoki cypresses. It's cold in winter and hot in summer, which is the reason for the trees' slow growth and the better wood quality with a dense structure. That's also the reason for the choice of hinoki for certain temple and shrine constructions. Long before the twentieth century, people cut down too many hinoki trees and the governor was worried about the eradication of this important tree. So he ordered the death penalty for cutting a tree, which was like 'one tree – one head'. Thanks to extensive reforestation there are no worries about a shortage of trees nowadays, although we shouldn't abuse Kiso hinoki until it disappears. It's one of the most beautiful trees in Japan." Takanori Kosegi

The traditional woodworking craft in Japan is kept alive by countless family-run businesses. Modern products made of wood are also usually still manufactured by small craft businesses. In Japanese society, stable business relationships with, for example, wood suppliers and other collaborators are established over many years. With this basis of mutual trust, products from outstanding raw materials can be manufactured to a high quality and reliably marketed in the long term.

"I was born in Kiso and raised there as well. My grandfather founded this factory and my father continues it. In my childhood I wasn't interested in it, it wasn't very cool. But now I'm glad to be doing the same thing that my parents did for so long. And it's awesome to have the chance to work with my family." Takanori Kosegi

A typical wood yard in the forest of the Kiso region.

Hideo Kosegi loads his transporter with sawn boards.

The workshop is located among fields, within sight of the Kiso River.

**Tree to Green**

**Tree to Green**

XV        XVI
XVII*    XVIII*

# TATEMOKU

**Manual work is,
in a park full of machines,
a filigree stew**

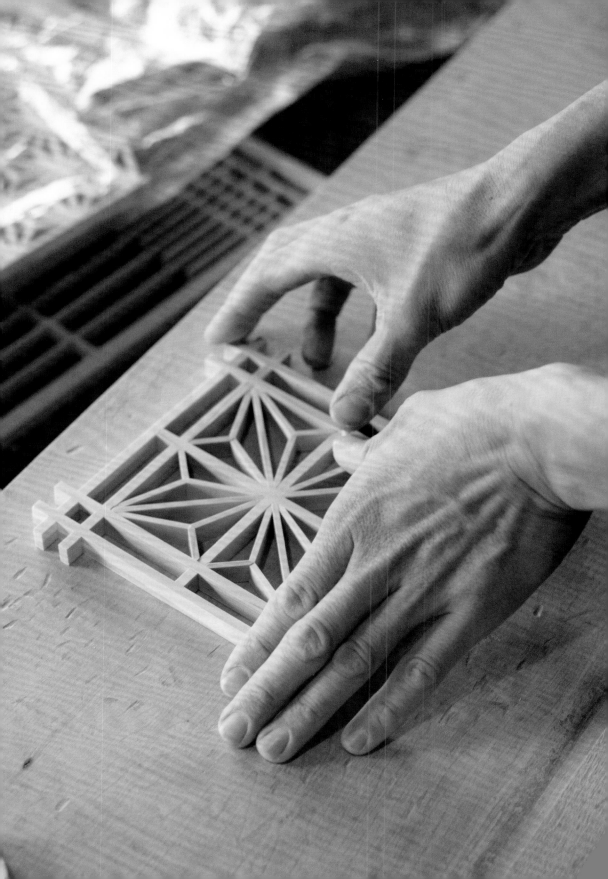

The roof construction, open on three sides, allows air to circulate. Tons of sawn timber is stacked in layers in all conceivable shapes and sizes up to the roof – old tree trunks, thick planks, narrow boards, thin strips, on pallets and in thick bundles on trolleys. In the TATEMOKU wood yard, the forklift truck has only a narrow aisle in which to manoeuvre.

Below the storage area, the workshop is full of a huge range of machinery. Like insect bones, a tangle of suction pipes pokes out from the dark ceiling, bending downwards into an almost impenetrable labyrinth of machines, pipes, hoses and cables. There are dozens of large, heavy milling machines, different types of saw, extraction systems and machines for planing, drilling, turning and grinding; nearby are shelves holding small pieces of equipment, manual tools, and various boxes and cartons. It requires respect from the visitor to get a good overview of this complex microcosm.

Half-finished workpieces are waiting to be completed on the few free surfaces. Among other interior projects, Takao and Toshihiko Tate and their team furnished the public library in the newly built Kiso Town Cultural Exchange Center for Tree to Green (see pages 144–155). In Japan, local craftspeople are often

Table in Kiso Town Library realized by TATEMOKU, 2017. The design for the project was by Tree to Green and Sekita Design Studio; woods used are Kiso hinoki cypress, zelkova, and Nara beech from the Kiso Valley.

involved in public projects. For example, TATEMOKU made the furniture for the local primary school.

TATEMOKU are also specialists in the custom-made *kumiko* (latticework) that can be found in *shōji* (the screens in sliding doors, windows, room dividers) and certain other surfaces of traditional Japanese homes. The intricate patterns made of precious wood are, along with the alcove (*tokonoma*) and wall shelves (*chigaidana*), an important part of Japanese furnishing culture. Combined with translucent paper for use on *shōji* screens and illuminated by the sun, they develop a special charm in the interplay of light and shadow and provide privacy at the same time.

All *kumiko* works are set in a wooden framework, within which is a uniform grid structure of narrow wooden strips. This forms the basic geometric pattern of repeating

triangles, squares, hexagons, and so on. These spaces are then filled with tiny, very precisely fitted wooden strip sections in patterns of varying complexity. All pieces are manufactured with such extreme precision that often no wood glue is necessary, because the lattice structures are given stability by the tension during assembly.

*Kumiko* designs are reminiscent of crystal structures, based on precise mathematical laws. Some of them are made of different coloured natural woods to lend further refinement to the design. In other styles, the strips might have not only different thicknesses but also waves and notches. Uniform patterns can form the background to abstract landscapes, or be interrupted by a few strong graphic elements. The intricacy and refinement of the pattern is a measure of the skill of the craftsperson.

*Kumiko* works today are mostly associated with traditional Japanese houses. But also many luxury boutiques, upscale lounge bars and upmarket hotels make use of the sophisticated geometric patterns. In modern interpretations, they can even look like abstract computer graphics and become a hip Japanese quote with an exclusive touch. Thanks to Japanese aesthetics and the rich Japanese ornamentation, they retain a timeless charm.

楯
木
工
製
作
所

I   The workshop consists of many buildings on different levels.
II   This *kakuasa* (square hemp) pattern is a typical *kumiko* design.
III   Able to call on a large number of machines, TATEMOKU can take on a wide variety of orders.

IV   Toshihiko Tate among his machines.
V   Sawn wooden planks are stored in the wood yard.
VI   Smoothing a wooden plank with a Japanese hand plane.

VII   The tops for the new tables of the Kiso Town Library are manufactured from solid wood.
VIII   A classic horizontal *kumiko* panel with the *asanoha* (hemp leaf) pattern based on regular hexagons.

IX   This complex lattice pattern for an interior combines several different *kumiko* details.
X   *Kumiko* can have widely varying styles, shapes and colours.

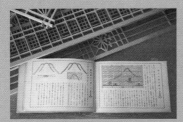

An old reference book with the model for the classic Mount Fuji motif.

The frame and inner parts of a *kumiko* section are assembled from identical parts to fit exactly together.

All sample pieces are based on the same principle of assembly.

楯高男 **Takao Tate** is the director and the second generation of the family business TATEMOKU, which manufactures high-quality wood furnishings in Nagiso, Nagano Prefecture. They are also specialists in *kumiko* latticework, which has a long-established role in traditional Japanese architecture.

楯敏彦 **Toshihiko Tate** is the grandson of the company founder and runs the daily business of TATEMOKU.

Founded in 1948, the company initially manufactured *magewappa*, steam-bent wood products originally from Odate in Akita Prefecture. Later, with around twenty to thirty employees, they produced house altars and *kumiko* latticework. At present, around seven employees manufacture wooden products for the company-owned shop in Tsumago, an important tourist destination not far away from the workshop, and construct newly designed interior projects for Tree to Green, among others.

Even in earlier centuries, highly specialized artisans for the

"Originally, I didn't know any craftsmen in Kiso but my parents have this factory, so they introduced me to some of them. One had had help from my grandfather in earlier days. We've had to find people that were able to adapt our newly designed products. My parents found some serious candidates for my company. Now I'm working with some people who even knew my grandfather or who know my parents, which is very important for a Japanese business relationship thanks to the shared roots between families or companies."

Quote from interview with Takanori Kosegi, co-founder of Tree to Green

production of complicated *kumiko* works served a market for wealthy owners of large manor houses. Especially in pre-industrial times, the lattice structures were associated with an enormous amount of craftsmanship. Dozens of *kumiko* patterns with different styles and varying degrees of difficulty were established over time. The structures decorate translucent *shōji* sliding door elements, narrow skylights, room dividers, wall designs and lampshades with their geometric patterns.

From the second half of the twentieth century, with the advent of modern woodworking machines, the precise manufacturing of regularly patterned strips became more affordable. However, the complexity of the pattern, the degree of irregularity, the number of small wooden parts and the amount of manual work still determine the effort that goes into a product and its resulting price – regardless of whether they are classic lattices or patterns based on modern design concepts.

Another popular traditional pattern, *rindo* (gentian), in a commissioned work.

On the main street of the old post town of Tsumago, TATEMOKU run their own shop.

A classic lampshade using *kumiko* with the *asanoha* pattern.

**TATEMOKU**

楯木工製作所

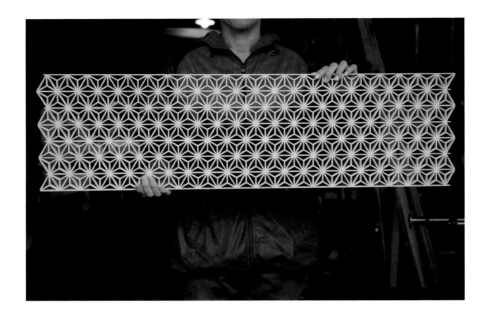

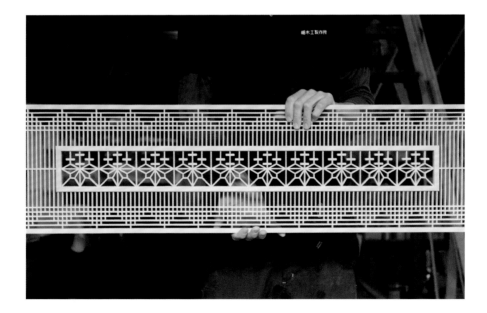

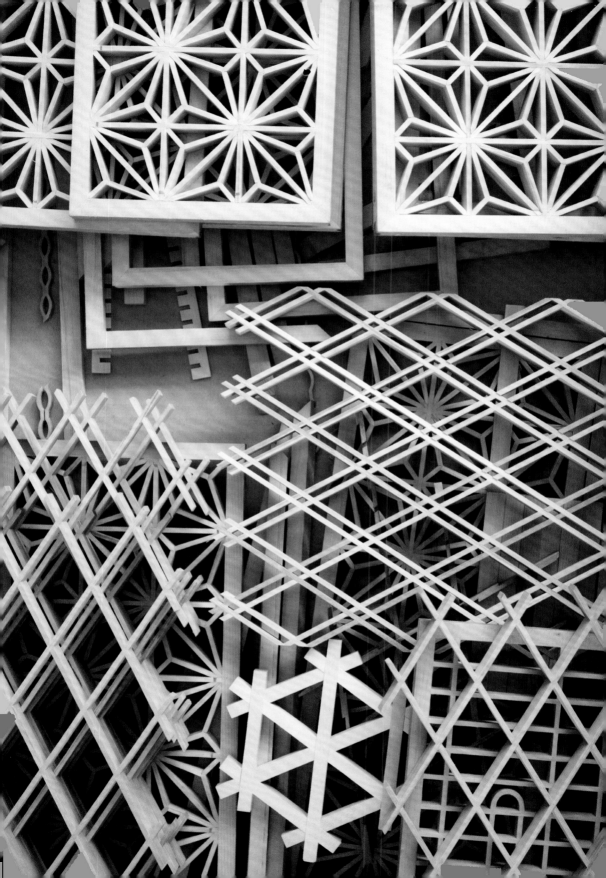

# Okekazu

**Little preciousness,
    hinoki and her sisters,
        grown for devotion**

Okekazu

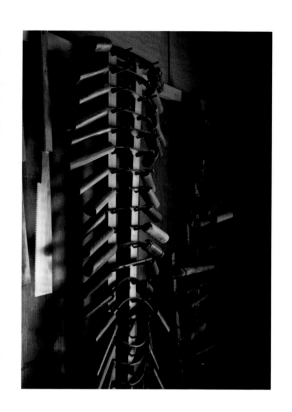

桶
数

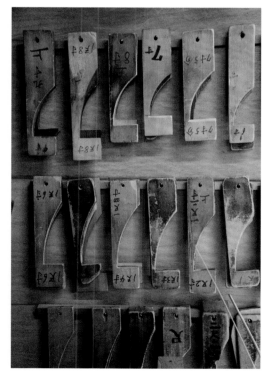

167

IV    V
VI    VII

**Okekazu**

Hot water steams in the bathtub, calm and compelling. The obligatory cleansing of the body with a soapy lather is welcome after an exhausting day, as is the repeated rinsing with warm water from a small wooden bucket. But both are only a foretaste of the slow gliding into the hot water in the tub, expertly carpentered from bright natural hinoki trunks. The wooden surfaces look slippery through the mirror-like water, but the feet find a natural grip. Everything feels soft thanks to the warmth of water and wood. One breathes out deeply when the whole body is immersed. The water settles and complete relaxation begins.

This is the primal Japanese pleasure, taking a bath in a tub made of calmingly scented hinoki. Okekazu have been manufacturing such tubs for Japanese hot spring spas (*onsen*) and bathhouses (*sentō*) for years, as well as bathtubs and washbasins for private use and traditional cooperage products (*oke*). They also produce a series of designer washbasins and a round, solid bathtub for the designer Ryu Kosaka. The tub is made from twenty 300-year-old hinoki cypresses and is ordered by luxury hotels or very wealthy individuals. The wood contains natural essential oils and retains its water-resistant properties over time.

The traditional repertoire of an *oke* maker is handmade wooden

Kesao Ito preparing huge curved staves of hinoki for one of the bathtubs for the "Furo Project".

barrels, tubs and buckets. The natural characteristics of the wood are exploited so as to avoid further protective treatment. Containers for cooked rice are mostly made of sawara wood because of its hygroscopic (moisture-absorbing) and simultaneously water-resistant properties. Water buckets for the Japanese bath are mostly made of hinoki or sawara, thanks to their water resistance. Examples made by Okekazu include a light Kiso sawara bucket with copper or stainless-steel hoops, or a version made of Kiso hinoki with hoops of

Finished solid wood bathtub for the "Furo Project" measuring approx. 1.4 m (4½ ft) in diameter. Design: Ryu Kosaka of A.N.D.

braided brass wire and a sloping top edge for one-handed use. They make both buckets for the lifestyle brand Kiso Lifestyle Labo by Tree to Green (see pages 144–155), as well as a round, three-legged stool for home use with the same materials. Kesao Ito and his son Takumi are also specialists in the making of barrels as tall as a person for the traditional production of Japanese food, such as miso paste made from fermented soya beans.

The physical way of working has hardly changed for centuries, and is based on the ergonomic tools and utensils adapted to each work step. The workbenches that are often used in woodworking are not used here. When processing the staves with drawknives, the cooper sits astride a sloping wooden plank (image V). Its end acts as a counterweight to a stomach guard tied to him, with the workpiece clamped in between. A special seat device held down by his body weight helps him to work the stave surfaces efficiently with curved planes. Often the craftsman's whole body serves as a universal bench vice while the workpieces are being processed.

As a demonstration of their abilities, they have set up a small bathroom in their workshop. Guests of the craft workshop might be invited to take a Japanese bath here at the end of the day – of course with a hinoki bucket and in a hinoki bathtub made by Okekazu.

桶
数

I The dense interior of the Kiso Valley's largely natural forest.
II The inside is smoothed with a round plane, while the workpiece is held steady by the craftsman's toes.
III In the foreground are some of the light water buckets used in Japanese baths, for Tree to Green's Kiso Lifestyle Labo.

IV Many of the drawknives and other tools formerly belonged to the grandfather.
V Takumi Ito processes staves for small buckets with a drawknife.
VI A gauge is used to check the correct angle of the stave edges.
VII Most tools are intended only for a specific diameter.

VIII Takumi Ito in the workshop, next to a stack of half-finished buckets.
IX Kesao Ito under the canopy of the workshop, where wood is often left to weather.
X The hoops for buckets and so on may be made of copper, brass or braided bamboo.

XI The three oval cut-out legs of the stool are reminiscent of a ceremonial tree-felling technique from Kiso used for the Ise Shrine. Design: Tree to Green.

Wood for containers is weathered for up to one year.

The staves are smoothed on the inside and outside with drawknives.

A long plane gives the edges the correct angle.

伊
藤
今
朝
雄
**Kesao Ito** runs the family business Okekazu in Agematsu, Nagano Prefecture, which uses traditional cooperage techniques to make wooden barrels and buckets (*oke*) for water and food, as well as solid wood bathtubs and basins for Japanese hot spring spas (*onsen*) and bathhouses (*sentō*). His father, Kazuma Ito, took him on as an apprentice in 1975 to teach him the art of making *oke*.

伊
藤
匠
**Takumi Ito,** the third generation, completed his woodworking training at the Agematsu Technical College in 2012, and continued his apprenticeship for several years in Kyoto with the well-known *oke* workshop Nakagawa Mokkougei. Since 2016 he has been working in the family business to deepen the subtleties of *oke* production.

The *onsen* buckets and bathtubs are partly created in collaboration with contemporary Japanese designers. For example, Tree to Green cooperate with Okekazu for

"Hinoki wood is somehow water-resistant, it has a good smell and it's anti-bacterial, so we use it for cutting boards, and it looks very soft. It's very Japanese and it's the most characteristic wood from the Kiso area. For centuries hinoki and sometimes sawara were preferred for the typical bathing stool, as well as for *oke* and other kitchen utensils. Now we use it for our kitchen and bathing products too, and we are also creating a hinoki crib as the smell can help in calming down babies. We try to make surprising products with a large variety of goods. Hinoki from Kiso is very characteristic for this region, and I think it is the best hinoki in Japan and even the world."

Quote from interview with Takanori Kosegi, co-founder of Tree to Green

some projects, as the company's founder, Kazuma Ito, and Takanori Kosegi's grandfather knew each other in earlier years.

Today's home of traditional Japanese cooperage made from sugi (Japanese cedar) is Akita Prefecture, but cooperage craftspeople can be found in other regions too. Owing to the abundance of equally suitable wood such as hinoki and sawara, the Kiso Valley is a perfect place for this craft. The traditional techniques and most of the tools used to make the wooden containers, such as drawknives and planes, were developed during the Muromachi period (1338–1573). Today's coopers' goods are still traditional commodities but now also include finely designed consumer goods with a modern touch. They are appreciated in Japanese cuisine, baths, and (in larger dimensions) traditional sake and miso production facilities.

Natural rice glue and bamboo plugs help to join the staves together.

The conical cylinders are held together with temporary wire hoops.

Upper and lower edges are smoothed with a knife and a piece of hardwood.

# Okekazu

桶
数

# Yamaichi Ogura Rokuro Crafts

**A deciphered growth
follows axial shaping
with tangential forces**

Yamaichi Ogura Rokuro Crafts

ヤマイチ小椋ロクロ工芸所

VIII   IX
X   XI

# Yamaichi Ogura Rokuro Crafts

The parking area next to the building is striking in its size – there is room for coaches. Around the sides lie massive tree trunks and thick sawn-off branches. The reason whole groups of tourists come to the small village of Hogami, at the end of a valley amid the dense forests of Kiso, is *Nagiso rokuro zaiku* – the traditional wood-turning craft of the area.

This is the site of Yamaichi Ogura Rokuro Crafts. The craftspeople employed by company owner Kazuo Ogura make up to 100 different product lines from solid hardwood pieces: vases, cups, saucers, plates, bowls, dishes, trays and various containers, from small to large, fine or robust. They use more than twenty different wood species, grown entirely in Japan.

The design for most of the pieces follows practical or traditional aspects. The wall thicknesses of larger objects remain easily graspable and above all solid. Large heavy bowls used for the making of soba noodles can have a diameter of up to 1 m (39 in.). But intricate design pieces can also be found among their works, such as a series of vases with an elegant twist in their proportions, to accentuate the beauty of a single flower. A series of disc-like wooden works forms a contemporary basis for *ikebana*, the Japanese art of flower

arranging. And for Tree to Green (see pages 144–155) they produce a series of off-centre plates, partially lacquered with coloured *urushi*, for the arrangement of *wagashi* (sweets) or fruits.

Common to all works is the accentuation of the natural beauty of the grain, the colour and the visible annual growth rings of each piece of wood. Retarded growth, burls, or even a bacterial infestation leading to discolorations in the wood, make every single tree exciting and individual. It was out of the ability to read the felled tree trunks that the art of *Nagiso rokuro zaiku* developed. With many years of experience, Kazuo Ogura only has to look at a trunk to recognize its inner structure and which part is suitable for which work. Special sawing and splitting methods are used to obtain as many workpieces as possible with interesting individual characteristics.

Kazuo Ogura accompanies the wood from its origin in the forest to the lacquering work. He even

Historical drawing of a lathe that was muscle-driven via ropes, *c.* mid-18th century.

attends the felling of the trees and chooses the best pieces. In the wood yard below the showroom and workshop, tons of valuable woods lie in tall stacks – thick unsawn trunks, tree slices sawn across the grain, slabs cut into blocks, boards sawn lengthwise, shorter beams and slats. Pre-machined semi-finished products in bowl shapes can also be found everywhere, stored on narrow wooden slats under the ceilings. Much patience is required, as the timber is usually seasoned for one to three years, up to ten for larger pieces, or even thirty with enough space and good ventilation.

After sufficient seasoning, the wooden blocks are machined on special lathes using up to twenty different turning chisels. Each craftsman forges his own tools in a small forge and sharpens them constantly during the work. The choice and use of the right tool, suitable for the wood, speed and workpiece, can be mastered only after a long period of learning. The turned products are processed with sandpaper and polished or varnished, often by wiping *urushi* into the wood (*fuki-urushi*), a technique that further highlights the beautiful grain and protects the objects. In the large showroom, customers can take a close look at all the pieces and pick them up before they drive back to the Kiso Valley.

ヤマイチ小椋ロクロ工芸所

I  Several cut trees lie on the edge of the parking lot to dry.
II  Finishing the surface of a large bowl with sanding paper. The craftsmen usually sit with their feet in a pit in front of the facing lathe.
III  Large tree slices are often left to season over several years.
IV  All objects are made from solid or pre-turned semi-finished products.

V  Rough-turned objects are piled up everywhere for drying, even in the wood-cutting workshop.
VI  Application of *urushi* to a tea caddy; a polyurethane lacquer protects other objects.
VII  Several finished trays made of different types of wood.
VIII  Each craftsman forges and sharpens his own turning tools.

IX  A small forge is sufficient for the chisels.
X  Small bowls made of (from top) keyaki, kuri, two other types of keyaki, and tochi wood.
XI  All objects are sanded inside and outside on the lathe.
XII  From left to right: Chiyoko Taniguchi, Masami Shibuya, Kazuo Ogura and Shizuko Kanbara.

XIII  Plate made of yamanarashi wood, partially painted with *urushi*. Design: Tree to Green.
XIV  UFO vases in keyaki, kurogaki and tochi wood, with red *urushi* and polyurethane lacquers.
XV  Examples of a series of vases made of sen and keyaki wood. Design: Hideki Nishiyama.

Heavy handsaws were still in use in the second half of the last century.

Kazuo Ogura's father saws a thick log by hand, around 1970.

Marking the shape to be sawn out of the block with a template.

小
椋
一
男

**Kazuo Ogura** runs the family business Yamaichi Ogura Rokuro Crafts, a wood-turning company in a valley in Nagiso, Nagano Prefecture, in the fifth generation. As a young man, he made up his mind to take over the company from his parents one day. Their work was successful and he wanted to continue the long family tradition.

The company manufactures various products of the local *Nagiso rokuro zaiku* from solid wood – mainly hardwood. Besides the lathed goods, it manufactures high-quality furniture ranging from Japanese living-room cupboards and chairs to large tables, all made with classic carpentry techniques from solid wood.

Around 1970 the turnery was still a relatively small business. However, the family realized the importance of premium presentation and built a large building with workshops, a shop space and adjacent large parking lot.

Including Kazuo Ogura, four craftsmen and two craftswomen master the process steps from selecting the wood and turning the

Wood from Japanese forests used by Yamaichi Ogura Rokuro Crafts:

Asada – Japanese hop hornbeam
Hōnoki – Japanese big-leaf magnolia
Ichii – Japanese yew
Ichō – Ginkgo
Kaede – Maple
Katsura – Katsura tree
Kaya – Japanese nutmeg
Keyaki – Japanese zelkova
Kihada – Amur cork tree
Koematsu – Heartwood of
Japanese pine
Kuri – Japanese chestnut
Kurogaki – Black persimmon
Kusu – Camphor tree
Kuwa – Mulberry
Mizume – Japanese cherry birch
Nara – Deciduous oak
Natsume – Jujube
Nire – Japanese elm
Onigurumi – Japanese walnut
Sen – Castor aralia
Shioji – Broadfruit ash
Tamo – Japanese ash
Tochi – Japanese horse chestnut
Yamanarashi – Japanese poplar
Yamazakura – Japanese cherry
Yanagi – Willow

full wooden block on the facing lathe to the finished, often *urushi*-lacquered, product. Three more employees take care of sales and administration. The company sells up to 90 per cent of its works direct to customers.

Japanese woodworkers particularly known for lathed plain-wood products are sometimes called *kijishi* (roughly, "wood grain master"), renowned for their expert woodworking skills and their in-depth knowledge of the properties of wood. It is said that their ancestors can be traced back more than 1,100 years.

Historically, one worker had to drive the simple lathes by muscle power, while another had to guide the turning tool. In the middle of the Meiji period (1868–1912), waterwheels brought kinetic energy, later replaced by electricity. The craft became considerably faster and easier. The laborious cutting of the massive logs with very large heavy handsaws and axes was later simplified by the invention of smaller bandsaws and chainsaws.

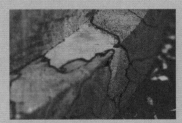

Bacterial discolorations in the tochi wood create beautiful patterns.

When pre-turned bowls are seasoned, the wood continues to release moisture.

The lathe chisel is often guided by a transverse beam.

ヤマイチ小椋ロクロ工芸所

ヤマイチ小椋ロクロ工芸所

# OTA MOKKO

**Colourful woods form
jointly patterned variety,
an abstract basis**

W ater flows past in the old Itabashi Yosui canal, built long ago as a private water supply. Beyond the canal, mint-green corrugated iron walls, rusted and weathered, enclose a partly covered inner courtyard. From a door to the left comes the smell of fresh wood shavings. To the right, a metal-clad sliding door allows a glimpse into a room lined with zinc. This was used for the mouse-proof storage of udon and soba noodles: this characterful building was an old noodle factory, and it is now the place where artisan Ken Ota produces modern *yosegi zaiku* marquetry under the name OTA MOKKO.

In *yosegi zaiku*, a traditional craft, abstract mosaics are assembled from small triangular, quadrangular, pentagonal, hexagonal and octagonal rods that are glued together to form a geometric pattern. Thin layers of end-grain wood are then sliced off and used to cover a variety of wooden objects. In a second *yosegi zaiku* technique, objects are worked from the full pattern block.

Ken Ota's concept is the refinement of everyday objects, which is why usability in the form of smooth radii and resistant varnishes is important to him. No less important are his original, contemporary patterns and exciting colour combinations. He covers trays, lunchboxes and bento boxes with the sliced mosaic layers. From the full block he makes card cases, writing instruments, buttons, coasters, bowls and sake utensils. He does not want to

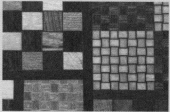

"Tsubaki", "Hiraori", "Marutsunagi" (from top) – three *yosegi zaiku* patterns made by OTA MOKKO.

completely reinvent the craft, but to expertly explore its potential.

*Yosegi zaiku* must be one of the most accurate and small-scale woodworking crafts, since you have to work to an accuracy of 0.1 mm, to avoid gaps or crooked patterns. This precision must be maintained in all approximately twenty work steps, from the planning of the pattern, through the sawing of the strips and slicing of the veneers, to the gluing of the products.

Ken Ota uses twenty-five beautiful, naturally coloured woods for his own production. Twenty-two of these originate from tree species in Japan and three from certified international sources. He is interested in woods that other artisans do not use. If possible, he inspects the entire log and gets it delivered as boards. The further cutting, sawing, splitting and peeling he does himself.

Each year OTA MOKKO develops a new abstract pattern of its own. In this context, symmetry sometimes plays a larger role, sometimes a less important one. "Hiraori" (plain weave) is the name of a pattern that looks woven. "Marutsunagi" appears like many connected circles, although they are sawn octagons. The "Yatara" (random pattern) has a rather rugged and lively look. "Tsubaki" (camellia) is reminiscent of camellia blossoms, and "Bara" is the name of the finely chiselled pattern inspired by rose petals. Each mosaic is formed only by the colours and grains of precious woods, which is perhaps the most important aspect.

At OTA MOKKO Ken Ota and his wife, Umi, form both a family and a craft team. She performs many steps in assembling the woods into patterns, helps in the shop and consults with her husband on ideas for new products. The trusting and honest contact between them works to their mutual benefit, as they are not bound by the traditional relationship of master and apprentice. In practice, they are a successful team of two like-minded people.

OTA MOKKO

I   The inner courtyard of OTA MOKKO's workshop in a former noodle factory in Odawara.
II   Different patterns are put together from prepared strips of natural coloured wood from various tree species.
III   The old workshop has a charming atmosphere.

IV   Ken Ota assembles boxes already covered with patterns at his workstation.
V   Attractive old *yosegi zaiku* end pieces lie on a low table.
VI   Ken Ota at the table where his wife often composes the patterns.
VII   Umi Ota at the door to the workshop store.

VIII   The carefully selected woods used for the patterns are naturally coloured.
IX   Where noodles used to dry, today valuable woods are stored.
X   The sake cups and the saucer are turned from the full block.

XI   The "Tsubaki" pattern on the box is inspired by camellia flowers.
XII   Lunchbox (*jūbako*) with different-sized "Hiraori" patterns in the bottom and lid.
XIII   The powerful "Bara" pattern on this bento box is inspired by rose petals.

Umi Ota assembles pattern blocks from which thin layers will later be sliced.

This "Hiraori" pattern is reminiscent of a woven structure.

Colour reference panels with various woods.

太田憲 **Ken Ota** produces under the name OTA MOKKO everyday objects with various wood colours and patterns, modern interpretations of the classical *yosegi zaiku* craft, in Odawara, Kanagawa Prefecture.

He learned the basics of woodworking at a vocational school in Saitama, where he encountered *yosegi zaiku* marquetry for the first time. Fascinated by its versatility, he decided to study the traditional craftwork in its region of origin, Odawara-Hakone. He found employment with Kiro, a well-known local *yosegi zaiku* producer, and moved with his family to Odawara in 2003. After eight years as a salaried craftsman he wanted to become independent, and founded his own studio, OTA MOKKO, in the same city. For several years his wife, Umi Ota, has performed many work steps, and is his creative partner at the same time. In 2015 they took the opportunity to open a larger workshop and craft store in a former factory.

Wood from international forests used by OTA MOKKO:
Purpleheart – Amaranth
Rosewood – Rosewood
Amoora – Mahogany

Wood from Japanese forests used by OTA MOKKO:
Makaba – Monarch birch
Urushi – Japanese lacquer tree
Enju – Japanese pagoda tree
Kenponashi – Japanese raisin tree
Jindai-nire – Subfossil elm
Raidenboku – Yellow catalpa
Ichō – Ginkgo
Shurizakura – Hokkaidō bird cherry
Akagi – Bishop wood
Nigaki – Quassia wood
Tamo – Japanese ash
Azukinashi – Korean mountain ash
Jindai-tamo – Subfossil Japanese ash
Kuwa – Mulberry
Kaede – Maple
Mizuki – Giant dogwood
Onigurumi – Japanese walnut
Ichii – Japanese yew
Kihada – Amur cork tree
Fujiki – Japanese yellowwood
Hōnoki – Japanese big-leaf magnolia
Yamamomo – Japanese bayberry

Listed according to order on image VIII (from front to back).

In the foothills of the Hakone valley, wood inlays have been produced for hundreds of years. The diversity of local tree species offers many design possibilities thanks to the natural colouring of their woods. The nearby Mount Fuji and numerous *onsen* (hot springs) in the idyllic valley have always attracted many travellers, who appreciate marquetry objects as souvenirs. There used to be about fifty specialized *yosegi zaiku* workshops in the region, of which only fifteen remain.

"Each workshop uses different woods. I am fascinated by woods that no one else uses. When I find a new type of wood that I like in one of my books, I ask several wood traders if they have it, and I will go there directly to take a look. Before buying, I want to see it with my own eyes because there are many individual differences in each wood log." Ken Ota

The sliced layers are glued onto wooden surfaces and assembled into small boxes.

A series of boxes in the making.

Some small offcuts from production.

**OTA MOKKO**

# Kazuto Yoshikawa

A beautiful mind,
    feels what is grown, worships nature,
        appreciates the origin

**Kazuto Yoshikawa**

吉川　和人

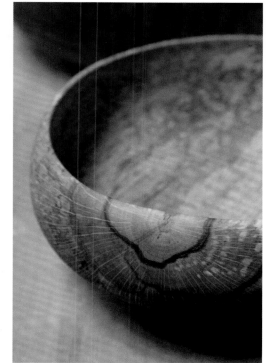

IV　V
VI　VII

# Kazuto Yoshikawa

An old seat, a handcrafted post-and-rung chair, a music stand made of rough wood, a weathered branch, another branch, a gorilla, an angel and the Grim Reaper stand on shelves built by Kazuto Yoshikawa on the back wall. The craftsman creates his pieces from solid wood in the workshop of a joinery in Tokyo – slender chopping boards with a beautiful grain, elegant spoons, slim drinking cups, plates, brooches, boxes and inspiring figures made from offcuts of wood.

Kazuto Yoshikawa is also inspired by Western design approaches, in interaction with Japanese aesthetics. On the one hand, he can draw on his work experience in an international designer furniture company in Tokyo. On the other hand, he is motivated by the work of pioneers such as French architect and designer Charlotte Perriand, with her special relationship to Japan and natural materials in general, or artists such as the painter Joaquín Torres-García, a propelling force of constructivism. Furthermore, Kazuto Yoshikawa is impressed by the creative power of the unconscious in the sometimes accidental and unintended paths of modern painting.

For his free works, he is interested in exceptional woods, woods with natural defects, such as bacterial stains and peculiarities in the grain. Every wood differs in colour, grain, smell and weight. It offers an intimate feeling that only genuine, natural materials such as leather,

For the wooden armchair "My Tree" made for the municipal library in Toyooka, Hyōgo Prefecture, Kazuto Yoshikawa was inspired by an essay from Kenzaburō Ōe that describes the relationship between trees and human spirits.

cotton and linen can have. For example, some wooden blocks for his turned bowls of Japanese oak often still have a residual moisture. Thus the wood keeps a rough surface, can still change form, and sometimes even cracks. So nature can still interfere in the design and remain visible in the works.

In his commissioned works, Kazuto Yoshikawa carefully selects characteristic tree species. The results are individual wooden furniture, beautiful sideboards, cupboards, tables or showcases with a modern design. He likes to use solid wood joints, as with classic Japanese furniture. He obtains his wood from wood markets in Kakamigahara and Takayama, Gifu Prefecture, sometimes even taking the trunks that others reject. From time to time he also uses urban trees that had to be felled for

reasons of age or construction work. They get a second life in a respectful encounter.

A particular concern in his work is the facilitation of a didactic approach, which becomes visible for example in a furniture project for Jiyu Gakuen school in Higashikurume, a suburb of Tokyo. The private school was established in 1921 and focuses in its curriculum on practical and basic experiences in daily life. The students grow their own vegetables and take care of the school's own forests in Saitama Prefecture. The school commissioned Kazuto Yoshikawa and fellow craftsmen to make new school furniture, 300 sets of desks and chairs, in a three-year project. Some of the students are involved in the project by watching how the trees are cut in a forest in Gifu Prefecture and by helping in some steps of the manufacturing process in the school's carpentry workshop. Their knowledge of the materials' origin leads to a deeper and essential understanding and appreciation of things.

In Kazuto Yoshikawa's opinion, mass-produced goods, fast food and fast fashion principally make life more comfortable, whereas life can actually be enriched by doing things with one's own hands – through the emotional connection between hand and heart. In this way, he wants to convey to people that there can be simple, original, even elementary forms of joy besides the high-tech entertainment possibilities in a megacity such as Tokyo.

吉川　和人

I   The stockyard of a wholesaler in Kakamigahara from which he obtains some of his wood.
II   Kazuto Yoshikawa at his lathe; in the background the shelf with objects.
III   He works with massive logs as well as long sawn boards.
IV   Examining an almost completed bowl.
V   The daylight from the skylights creates a beautiful studio atmosphere.
VI   The turned works are created on a universal lathe with a tailstock.
VII   By emphasizing the individual grain, the item's natural origin as a tree remains visible.
VIII   Some of the slim cutting boards in different processing stages.
IX   Simple pieces of wood can also tell whole stories.
X   Kazuto Yoshikawa thinks beyond borders.
XI   Cutting boards made of horse chestnut, walnut and cherry.
XII   The figures made of offcuts of wood stimulate everyone's imagination.
XIII   Plate, cups, bowl, brooches, spoons and dessert knives made of various woods.
XIV   Bowls turned from Japanese oak, with intentional cracks and deformations.

Kazuto Yoshikawa carved this spoon for his mother at around the age of ten.

From this part of a tree from a Tokyo street, a bowl is to be created.

Spoons in various forms from a wide range of woods.

吉
川
和
人

**Kazuto Yoshikawa** is an artisan in Setagaya, Tokyo, who exhibits his wooden everyday objects and sculptures, and manufactures sophisticated solid-wood furniture for customers. He is successfully represented by Japanese and international galleries with his free works. Originally he studied commercial science at Keiō University in Tokyo, and then worked for more than twelve years for Cassina IXC, the Japanese distributor of the famous Italian designer furniture.

"I like wood that is not plain and clean. I like using more rustic wood with an irregular grain, which reminds me that the wood once had a life as a tree. Wood is different from ceramic and iron. It is a biotic material. The factors that I cannot control, like irregular grain, sometimes give my works a sense of being alive."

Raised in the rural region of Fuku-shima, Kazuto Yoshikawa spent a lot of time as a child playing with wood and its origin, trees. In 2011, confronted with the nationwide effects of the devastating Tōhoku earthquake, he steered his path in a different direction, and started to study the basics of woodworking at a vocational school in Gifu Prefecture. Since then he has followed his true calling, the creation of wonderful things made of wood with his own hands, following the premise of a respectful use of natural resources. Furthermore, he would like to pass on his ideas to people in his workshops.

One of the essential tasks of a craftsman making artistic work like Kazuto Yoshikawa is to find buyers for the self-initiated works. The number of suitable galleries is limited and talented artists are numerous. By combining outstanding works, his personal concept, and a talent for presentation, he achieved his first successes. Subsequently, sponsors were found who also introduced him to a wider audience.

"I feel people in the world are getting fed up with industrial mass-produced things which are made just in terms of competitive pricing. They enrich our lives in terms of conven-ience, but they cannot enrich our lives essentially. Things made by hand have a feeling of one's heart because the hands and heart are directly connected. [...] I want to show my children the way I work. There are many choices for everyone in how to live and how to earn money, but I want to teach them to try things. It's easy to enter a com-pany and have a salary. But to make money with your skills in making things you like is not easy, to be independent is not easy. I want to show them different options for life."

Some quick sketches for block figures made from wooden offcuts.

Part of Jiyu Gakuen (Freedom School) in a suburb of Tokyo.

Just before finishing the first new school desks for Jiyu Gakuen.

## Kazuto Yoshikawa

吉川　和人

X

# Kazuto Yoshikawa

吉川　和人

# Koichi Onozawa

The clod of earth rose,
    hidden deep in the coarse ground
        a fine spirit emerges

**Koichi Onozawa**

小野澤 弘一

V    VI
VII   VIII

**Koichi Onozawa**

Numerous large and small rice fields fill the gaps between the driveways to isolated farmsteads. Hidden behind high trees, some flat sheds are grouped around a house, whose bright blue tiled roof shines out between the branches. In the corner of a nearby equipment shed there is a small plywood booth, equipped with a simple sliding door, a potter's wheel, a table made of thick beams, a wall shelf and an old office swivel chair. This is the ceramics studio of Koichi Onozawa, next to the house where he lives with his wife. In a second shed is the large gas kiln in which he fires his works.

He does not need much to work. Calm and serene, he wants to create nothing less than something as great as nature, that touches every human being, regardless of their cultural background. He aims for his works to be simple and powerful, like those of earlier times – such as the ceramics excavated from a nearby burial mound (c. 700 CE) – but also modern. Ultimately, his works are at the same time ageless, earthy and somehow immaterial.

Even today Koichi Onozawa uses the same clay sourced from the soil of Seto, Aichi Prefecture, with which he learned the subtleties of ceramics during his studies. He mixes the clay from 20-kg (44-lb) blocks of red-brown and grey-green clay. The mineral differences are perceptible in the characteristic texture of his works. Cutting the blocks several times, he puts

Urushi tree, part of a reforestation campaign supported by Koichi Onozawa.

together a three-dimensional chessboard and mixes everything into a homogeneous brown clay mass during the exhausting wedging process. For him, this clay is like a partner whom one has to get to know well before going through life together.

From it he forms object-like bowls and elegant vases with thin walls and delicate edges. At first, everything is created symmetrically on the potter's wheel, smoothed by shaped wooden gauges, a leather strip or an old credit card. Many pieces – cylindrical pots, bulbous vases with narrow openings, wide bowls – are sanded down after drying to further reduce the wall thickness and smooth the outside.

Koichi Onozawa pushes some of his beautiful and intrinsically symmetrical bowls into asymmetry immediately after throwing. In others, he makes a sharp indent or curve inwards or outwards. Like the vases, the bowls often have very small bases. Inspired by the above-mentioned grave goods, which were created without bottoms, simply to be buried with the dead, he wants to give them fragility, instability and nervousness, a feeling of insecurity. These pieces are expressions of his artistic sensibility, in contrast to some of his other works, which are beautiful pared-down ceramics for everyday use.

After being fired in the gas kiln, the works are a warm grey, interspersed with small bright dots and white scratches, invoking the beauty of nature. The pieces have a smooth, soft feel. Some of them are additionally lacquered in red or black *urushi*; or he applies silver tin powder to them, so that every imperfection becomes visible. You can feel how thin even the larger bowls are by their harmonious and bell-like sound when you accidentally strike one, and it is easy to worry that they will break. But the material is solid, and you wish them the same long life as those undamaged grave goods. Koichi Onozawa hopes that they will touch the hearts of people worldwide, functioning, as he puts it, "beyond time, space and all differences".

小
野
澤
弘
一

I   The gas kiln in the shed is fired by several gas cylinders.
II   Koichi Onozawa in the studio before wedging two types of clay.
III   The cylindrical vases have been additionally painted with coloured and clear *urushi*.

IV   The ceramicist forms a small bowl out of a clay cone in his characteristic way of throwing.
V   A dried bowl is subsequently sanded to smooth its surface.
VI   The former tool shed is the ideal studio, with ample space.

VII   The potter's wheel is of course the most important tool of a ceramicist.
VIII   His works are perfect for a classic Japanese wall niche (*tokonoma*).
IX   Koichi Onozawa in his studio.

X   A series of small, irregularly shaped bowls.
XI   A bowl and a large vase treated with *urushi* and metal powder; the smaller vase is untreated.
XII   Detail of a vase surface refined with metal powder.

The clay must be powerfully wedged before it is used for pottery.

The wall thickness of a bowl is reduced with simple tools.

A leather-hard bowl is bent into an asymmetrical shape.

小
野
澤
弘
一

**Koichi Onozawa** is a successful studio ceramicist from Nakagawa, Tochigi Prefecture. He originally comes from Tokyo, where he studied economics, but after graduating he wanted to do something that he really loved. Thanks to his interest in ceramics, he decided to continue his education at a well-known ceramic school in Tajimi City, Gifu Prefecture, from which he graduated in ceramic design in 2008.

During his time in Tajimi, Koichi Onozawa became inspired by ceramics from the Momoyama period (1573–1603) and by Korean works to create his decorative objects, such as vases or object-like bowls. Since 2011 he has lived with his wife, Noriko, in rural Nakagawa, where the local tradition of pottery for rice grown in the region has inspired him to also create more practical bowls and plates. In nearby Ōtawara, Japan's earliest archaeological excavation activities revealed artefacts from the Kofun period (c. 300–700 CE) that equally fascinate him.

He wants his works to delight as many people as possible, regardless of nationality, language, religion and skin colour. He feels the equality of people in their core, connected by sensation and emotion when looking at beautiful things.

For ceramicists, and for Japan's craftspeople in general, it is increasingly important to be seen abroad and to travel to other regions of the world. This is both a task and a necessity, enabling one to learn from other cultures and convey common values, ideally through one's own work.

"I also would like my work to be my means of communication, by taking my work outside Japan, overseas, and getting other people with other cultures, different backgrounds, different languages, to see it. If my work can impress them somehow, I would feel very happy."

"The reason why some of my pots have a very narrow foot is to give them a sense of uncertainty or nervousness. They look unstable. The inspiration for that style actually came from the design of ancient pottery. The potters back then used to make them purely to be buried with the dead body. Those pots often lacked bottoms and had a hole instead. […] In this region there are quite a few ancient grave sites around and a lot of pottery is excavated. To me it's a miracle that pots that old could survive until now, and it touches me. I also feel a lot of energy from these old pots. I would like to create my work with the same level of energy."

The inside of a bowl is scraped out to reduce the wall thickness.

Tin powder is dusted onto damp *urushi* with a soft brush.

Wiping out the metal powder creates an attractive surface.

## Koichi Onozawa

小野澤 弘一

小野澤　弘一

# Shozo Michikawa

Forceful distortion,
   shifted axes in moist clay,
      beautiful power

**Shozo Michikawa**

道川　省三

IV

**Shozo Michikawa**

Tiles used to be produced here, in these low wooden buildings with broken bits of ceramic on the floor and everything a little crooked. Frosted glass windows let subdued light into a small room in the old factory. Curiously twisted objects stand on boards, shelves and low tables made of coarse planks. Labouring hands have left traces of clay everywhere. Shozo Michikawa is deeply rooted in this place, his first studio, where he has worked for more than forty years.

This is where his unique ceramic objects are created, full of tension and elemental power. Frozen in the moment of rotation, they seem to be a visualization of time itself. A combination of geometric form and basic principles of ceramic design, they are the artist's solution to squaring the circle.

He achieved this mode of artistic expression through trial-and-error and his constant energy. Shaping with vertical slices, horizontal division into blocks, rotation around the vertical axis. A cavity is formed inside and widened. Slow torsion of the blocks, with measured force, stretching and twisting. The outer skin ruptures. The opening is closed, everything turned upside down, a hole made. Dynamic shaping of the upper side. Inspection. Shozo Michikawa does not even need eight minutes for the whole process.

It is a concentrated process that he executes with great energy and a goal in mind. The combination of chance, strength and slowness allows Shozo Michikawa to express a controlled impulse, the result being an imperfect dynamic

A few examples of Shozo Michikawa's worldwide exhibitions, demonstrations and workshop activities (from top to bottom): 2016 at the New Century Crafts Museum, Seto; 2016 in Faenza, Italy; 2005 in the Forbidden City in Beijing, China.

roughness. All he does is assist the clay in reaching its own final shape, retaining its character.

Similarly, during firing, Shozo Michikawa cedes control to the elements. The wood fire in the *anagama* (cave kiln) takes on a life of its own. Ash swirls up and affects the surfaces of often combined glazes. Natural ash glaze in red-brown-green, white *kohiki* glaze, sometimes with dark iron sprinkles, blistering *shino* glaze. Some

pieces from the *anagama* are fired a second time in the gas kiln, and vice versa, aiming for intentional errors, glossy and matt areas, or colour changes – for example by refiring objects in large saggars (ceramic boxes) partly filled with charcoal, colouring the surface black, or by partially adding silver glazes. Shozo Michikawa often pursues such contrasting moments, and still everything is in balance.

All works receive a hole in the top. This is his way of giving them a function and identity, turning a piece of clay into an object. Tall sculptures are mostly vaselike. Small objects sometimes have a lid, like the water containers for the tea ceremony (*mizusashi*). Pot objects have lids and handles. But even his bowls are rarely used as such. The expressive shape and glaze make them independent, they need no content.

Overall, Shozo Michikawa is a very youthful person, restless, constantly communicating. His morning power-walk through nature is his source of inspiration. Twisted old trees, cracked bark, clods of earth, plants, a lake. He lets himself be guided by the energy, by the feeling on the spot, by the dynamics of the moment. Cumulated nature in clay. Shozo Michikawa himself calls it "Nature into Art".

His manner and objects also convinced Anita Besson (1933–2015), whom he met on his first trip to London. The important gallery owner and collector of ceramic art promoted and connected him worldwide. This was the foundation of his international success. In 2017, he celebrated the fortieth anniversary of his work as a ceramicist.

道 川 省 三

I    Clay tiles are embedded vertically in the ground to reinforce it.
II    Shozo Michikawa uses wire to separate a finished bowl from the potter's wheel.
III    Interior view of the studio with the table for wedging clay.

IV    Vertically twisted small vase object with natural ash glaze.
V–XII    Post-processing of a bowl with a scraper. A finished piece is ready to dry. The ceramicist's liveliness and joy often comes out in his work.

XIII    Shozo Michikawa in the studio at the potter's wheel; some works are already drying in the background.
XIV    Impression of the studio with some pieces in white *kohiki* glaze.

XV    Covering the object with charcoal during firing colours its surface black.
XVI    Three works on a low table in his house.
XVII    Detail of a strongly twisted work with natural ash glaze.

Moist clay is easily cut into shape with wire.

It is important to centre the clay block on the potter's wheel.

The dynamic shape develops within a few minutes.

道
川
省
三

Shozo Michikawa initially studied economics in Tokyo. After graduating, he worked for a company for two years while taking pottery classes in the evening. He was fascinated by the experience of creating something himself. Soon he decided to settle with his wife, Masae, in Seto, Aichi Prefecture, to dedicate himself solely to the work as studio ceramicist.

After a phase of making everyday pottery, Shozo Michikawa focused on art pieces. He now exhibits in galleries and museums worldwide and demonstrates his creative process on the potter's wheel in celebrated live performances. His works often recall the natural elements of Hokkaidō, where he grew up, with its forests, volcanoes and lots of snow.

In 2011 he co-founded the biennial International Ceramic Art Festival in idyllic Sasama, Shizuoka Prefecture, where young Japanese and international ceramicists can present to and inspire each other. Here he built his own *anagama*

"I don't believe in teachers, I don't believe in books. I always try, try by myself, and through this I can understand. Other people understand through books, but I need to try things by myself. Of course, it is impossible to throw triangular shapes. Therefore, I make a triangular or square block and put it on the wheel. [...] I'm more interested in how the clay changes when it is stretched or bent, and in its different, broken textures. It's like continuously talking with the clay. I don't like to always have control over everything. So when I start a work and see that the sculpture evolves in a different way than I might have imagined, I find it very interesting. In a way, I just help the clay find its shape."

(cave kiln), which he uses about twice a year for firing his works.

Centuries ago, ceramic styles, glazes and firing techniques from China and Korea were taken up in Japan and developed, especially under the influence of the Japanese tea ceremony. Unique styles and objects emerged, one of the main reasons for the worldwide reputation of Japanese ceramicists. Today, it is not always easy for ceramicists to sell their works, which makes it even more important to develop a distinctive individual style.

"Many terms in the ceramic world are Japanese words, like *raku*, *shino*, or other glazes. This is a mutual language that everybody knows. I myself also started in a very functional way, but it changed because at some point I felt like a businessman who had to take care of many orders."

A striped pattern is created on the clay using a ridged roller.

The clay is divided into blocks while a stick is inside.

The twist occurs when the stick counteracts the disc rotation.

## Shozo Michikawa

道川　省三

**Shozo Michikawa**

# Toru Hatta

**Packed in masonry
works awaiting wood fire,
random ashes fly**

An assortment of clay items stand on a long table under a corrugated iron shelter in Sakai, south of Osaka. The plates, bowls, cups, jugs and large vases are covered with a layer of glaze and waiting to be fired. By the table is an impressive brick structure. A smooth, rounded roof is supported by walls of sooty stones. In its cracked surface are four spyholes blocked by peculiar ceramic plugs. This is Toru Hatta's *makigama* (wood-fired kiln).

The whole family in the newly built house in Tondabayashi.

The studio ceramicist throws his pieces quickly and concentratedly on the potter's wheel. In the style of the *mishima* inlay technique, originating in Korea, he carves his characteristic patterns into some of them. These are then filled with a pale slip. Other pieces get a waved edge. The glazes of works with less unusual shapes will obtain their individual flaws during the wood firing. Some works are created in a combination of different techniques and styles.

Nature plays an active and creative role in Toru Hatta's ceramic series by provoking randomness in the process. For example, he sometimes digs clay himself, has it processed and then makes pottery with it.

But the most elaborate way of involving chance is definitely the use of a wood fire, in the *makigama* he built. He fires about ten or eleven times a year, which is very time- and material-consuming. Other ceramicists often team up to share a kiln and split the cost of the wood. It is also a good opportunity to meet and have a chat while taking care of the firing process.

At first, about 200 pieces of work are stacked closely together in the kiln, which rises up at the rear. The decisive factor for the glaze result is the position of a piece – whether it is at the top or the bottom, at the front or the back. The complex interaction of fire, ash and minerals in the clay is never completely under control. The type of wood also plays a role.

Before lighting a small fire at the stoking hole, a short prayer is recited. Wood is added quickly, while dense smoke escapes from the cracks in the kiln. Many hours later Toru Hatta removes the spherical plugs from the spyholes, whereupon the fire flames out like a welding torch. The kiln now radiates an unbelievable heat, which has to be controlled and further raised.

The next morning the spyholes are veritable flamethrowers. It is a mystical scene with a dragon-like fire-breathing kiln. Every few minutes throughout the day, wood is thrown in. On the second evening the crafts-man fishes a glowing test piece from a small opening. Again, loads of wood are thrown in from the front and the sides. Inside, ash whirls up and lies on the vitrifying glaze, creating intended flaws.

At night the digital thermometer finally shows the required 1,280 °C (2,336 °F), after thirty-six hours of continuous heating. Now the heat has to be held steady for a few more hours. In the morning, the front opening of the kiln is temporarily bricked up and all holes are sealed. After another thirty-six hours of cooling down, it is clear that the batch was successful, as beauty emerges from the ashes and the fire.

八田

亨

Toru Hatta sometimes makes objects based on ritual Haniwa figures from the Kofun period (*c.* 300–700 CE).

I   Above the rooftops of Tondabayashi.
II   Toru Hatta stacks the last pieces in his *makigama* before firing.
III   The ceramicist pro-duces a series of bowls for his *mishima* series.
IV   The soot-stained side of the *makigama*.
V   Flames come out of the kiln, while the fire rages inside.

VI   Toru Hatta in his big workshop next to the kiln.
VII   The ceramicist and a helper stoke the fire on the second night.
VIII   A Shinto priest holds a ceremony to bless the gas kiln prior to the first firing with this new facility.

IX   Toru Hatta lights the fire for the first firing with the gas kiln in his private house.
X   You can see the extreme way in which the firestorm in the *makigama* changed the glaze on the vase.
XI   Parts of his *shirokake* and *mishima* series, and bowls with black glaze.

XII   Toru Hatta's *mishima* ceramics are mostly grey with a light pattern.
XIII   Sake cups and plates from the wood fire. Unglazed spots (*me-ato*) are intentional and come from the way the pieces were stacked in the kiln.

Throwing bowls with the "cow-tongue" tool (*gyūbera*) made of pine.

Carving his characteristic *mishima* pattern on a turntable.

The pattern is characterized by diagonal lines running in opposite directions.

八
田
亨

**Toru Hatta** is a successful studio ceramicist who lives and works in Tondabayashi, Osaka Prefecture and makes *mishima* ceramics and other types of pottery. Allowing the randomness of nature is an important part of his working approach. His modern ceramic series are partly based on classical examples.

He studied architecture at Osaka Sangyo University and attended pottery courses at the same time. His first job was at the Maishima Pottery Museum in Osaka. Here he was able to gain further experience in the processing of certain types of clay and glazes, and in the use of wood firing in *anagama* kilns.

Toru Hatta runs a studio in Sakai, south of Osaka, where he gives courses for hobby ceramicists and fires his own pieces in his *makigama* kiln. In order to be closer to his wife and their four daughters, he set up a studio annexe to their newly built house in Tondabayashi, with a potter's wheel, a large gas kiln and lots of daylight.

"There is a craftsman that I greatly admire who makes a special kind of tray by carving it from a single piece of wood. Some years ago, he had a stroke and was unable to move one half of his body. Recently, he actually said that it was a good timing for him because in a way he felt that he had become too good at his craft. He feels that because he can only use one hand when working now, he is able to make more interesting work than he had before. Talking to him made me realize that doing work very meticulously and becoming perfect at your craft actually causes something to be lost in the process. So, for example, when you use clay that is difficult to shape, the work can be more interesting."

Pottery for everyday use is still produced in numerous regions and styles using handcrafted methods. There are countless individual studio ceramicists as well as larger family-owned craft businesses with several employees. Making a living as a ceramicist is only possible in Japan if one can successfully develop a signature style. The longevity of handicraft products, the huge historical heritage of craftsmanship, and industrially produced goods from Asia do not make it easy for young ceramicists to survive in the first years of their careers.

"I would like to work on my projects as an integral part of living. Ideally, when I woke up in the morning and brushed my teeth, I could just start throwing on the wheel immediately. And I have four small children: I would also like to have as much time as possible to be close to my family."

A glowing test piece taken out of the kiln indicates the state of the glaze.

The temperature is monitored at two points in the furnace.

Fire comes out of the chimney, which can be monitored with a mirror.

**Toru Hatta**

八田 亨

**Toru Hatta**

八田亨

X

**Toru Hatta**

# Kasamori | 000

**Designed with delight,
from noble yarn created,
lovely compliments**

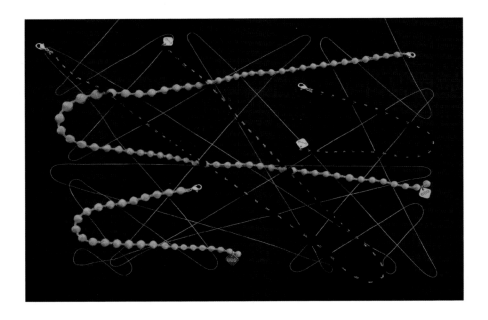

The staff meet each other in the narrow office corridor on Monday morning, while getting their duties for the week. At the weekend an urgent order was still running on the machines, the refinement of haute couture designs created by an avant-garde fashion label. The brand showed them a few days later at its fall/winter show during Paris Fashion Week.

The confidence of the fashion labels is evidence of the technical skill and innovative spirit of Kasamori, an embroidery specialist in Kiryū, Gunma Prefecture. In 1877 the former silk yarn merchants became a family business for weaving silk *obi* (kimono sashes). From the 1960s, the company once again transformed itself into a specialist for contract embroidery.

Embroidery was also strongly influenced by Jacquard looms. Their inventor, Joseph-Marie Jacquard, started a technical revolution with the use of punch cards. In this way, endless patterns of any complexity could be woven on the same looms. Later, this also enabled the automation of embroidery technology.

Kasamori's artistry captivates above all with its virtuoso use of computer-controlled technology and all its possibilities, through the embroidery programming of Fujiko Okada and her colleagues. About a dozen high-tech multi-head embroidery machines from a Japanese

Traditional entrance gate to the Kasamori workshop building.

manufacturer convert the program code, some with more than ten embroidery heads, up to twelve simultaneously usable yarns or yarn colours, and even sequins and other special features if required.

With methods such as *sagara*, cord, scallop, border and stitching embroidery or techniques such as chain stitching, hemstitching, cutwork and pleating, they strive to implement the customers' designs as accurately as possible. They rely on a combination of highly specialized services paired with a wealth of ideas. Thanks to the joy of finding good solutions and the understanding of technology and systems, the company has been able to reinvent itself several times. At the same time the owner, Yasutoshi Kasahara, feels a great responsibility towards his approximately thirty employees and their families.

With Yoichi Katakura, Kasamori was able to find an ideal creative

partner. Observing his mother's knitting work and his grandfather's origami art from a young age, he was fascinated by the abilities of human hands. His thirst for knowledge later led him to Europe and back to Japan with a degree in textile design. Always restlessly switching between machines, computers and sketchpads, he combines mathematical/technical skills with a creative desire to design.

The joy of experimenting culminated in the invention of their own patented technique, which they call Kasamori lace, and which led to the development of three-dimensional embroideries consisting only of yarn both inside and outside. This is particularly effective in the form of balls with embroidered connectors between them, from which the first embroidered line of jewelry was created. The pleasantly lightweight, easy-care materials and fresh colours proved immediately appealing, and customers did not have to worry about metal allergies.

Today, several lines are offered in various shapes and colour combinations and in exclusive materials such as fine silk or metallic yarns. Kasamori distributes the original jewelry under its own brand 000 (Triple O). The name stands for the start of something newly created, almost from scratch.

笠
盛
|
O
O
O

Production of silk-linen yarn at TOSCO's factory in Mihara, Hiroshima.

Sketching the design of a new necklace.

Detail of a thread running through the embroidery needle tip.

笠原康利 **Yasutoshi Kasahara** runs the company Kasamori in Kiryū, Gunma Prefecture, an embroidery specialist that emerged from a history of weaving high-quality kimono sashes (*obi*) since 1877. He is the family's fourth generation of craftsmen and grew up in the knowledge that one day he would continue the business.

片倉洋一 **Yoichi Katakura** moved to London after graduating in engineering. There he gained a BA in Textile Design from Chelsea College of Arts in 2003. He then worked on commission for haute couture houses in Paris and for a fabric producer in Switzerland. Back in Japan in 2005, he found in Kasamori a company that combined creativity and craftsmanship in one place.

With the design department that Yoichi Katakura set up, Kasamori developed its own technique for embroidering three-dimensional objects. The result was an original line of jewelry made of yarn, for which the brand 000 (Triple O) was founded in 2010.

Owing to the closure of Japan against external influences and goods from the 1630s onwards, for more than 200 years Japanese manufacturers produced practically for their own population alone. Thus, clothing styles and craftsmanship could evolve independently, be refined and continue to exist long after the opening of the country. With the advent of Western clothing and the industrial growth of neighbours in Asia, textile manufacturers in Kiryū and other regions had to reorient themselves in the long term.

"After the Second World War, the economy was growing. According to my father, *obi* sales went well, and my father and his brothers accounted for 30 per cent of *obi* sales in the Kiryū area. Gradually, people changed to Western-style fashion, and we shifted to the embroidery business because of the decrease in kimono use in the 1960s." Yasutoshi Kasahara

"I was looking for a job in a small company with a workshop rather than a famous design studio in Tokyo. I believe that design cannot be separated from making. Another reason why I came to Kiryū is that there is a famous weaving master, Junichi Arai. I am a big fan of his creation in terms of mixing technology and traditional craft techniques. [...] 000 means to go back to the start, like painting on a fresh new canvas. We try to ignore what we did for the previous 140 years as an embroidery and *obi* maker. I wanted to create a necklace like a pearl made of only silk thread with embroidery. After thousands of tests with engineer Miss Okada, we finally succeeded in making 3D balls." Yoichi Katakura

The fast machines embroider the necklaces on a special fleece.

Of course, all pieces are washable by hand.

Applying the clasps branded with the 000 logo.

# Kasamori | 000

笠盛 — ○○○

241

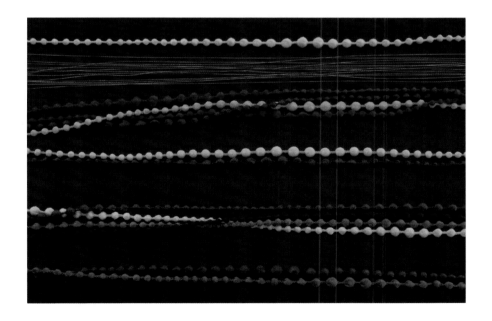

# tamaki niime

**The entire rainbow,**
        **warp, weft, warp, weft, and over again,**
            **arises in fluffiness**

**tamaki niime**

The buildings are dominated by white elements. Many machines in the hall are also sprayed white. The noise they make is the music of industrialization and an exciting look back into the technical evolution of weaving. It is also the conceptual core of the label of the textile artist Tamaki Niime, dominated by analogue mechanics, punch cards and many yarns. The brand, "tamaki niime", bears her own name.

Made of dark steel with a belt drive, ideal for slow speeds and low yarn densities, her first two looms, built in 1965, are still in use. On them she developed her vision of *Banshū ori*, yarn-dyed fabrics from Nishiwaki, Hyōgo Prefecture. Airy and fluffy, woven in all shades of colour, no two fabrics are the same. With a wonderfully soft handle, the original shawls became a great success. The brand now designs, manu-factures and sells a wide range of shirts, trousers, children's clothing, bags and denims, while Tamaki Niime constantly creates. Preferably right at the loom.

By using old weaving techniques, she turns the technical development upside down. Unexpected colour changes breathe cheerful sponta-neity. Machines no longer needed elsewhere have their second spring here, creating jobs where they disappeared long ago. Instead of producing large quantities, she focuses on quality, created without haste and with local inspiration – her constantly evolving experiment.

For Tamaki Niime, the looms in the workshop are like an empty canvas facing the first brushstroke. None of them dating from after 1983, all are controlled by punch cards, within which the weaving patterns are coded. There are also

Tamaki Niime on a veranda of her large workshop building.

facilities for spinning and dyeing yarns, and modern flat and circular knitting machines. All around the hall walls are countless numbers of colourful yarn spindles stored on open shelves, like a finely grad-uated colour spectrum. It is this colourful cheerfulness and the team members, most of whom are dressed in the own label, that make this place so likeable. They are like one big family.

A few years ago, the company began the ecological cultivation of cotton, which is now spun into their own yarns, dyed and woven into certain fabrics. They want to strengthen local production and encourage farmers to grow the old crop again, and achieve full trans-parency in the materials they use in the near future.

The holistic concept shows in a sympathetic way how to lead a brand to success, above all with respect for nature and its resources, for the people and their region. Tamaki Niime succeeds by being contemporary, together with a careful reorientation of traditional methods, and a great deal of courage, joy in experimenting and adher-ence to her own ideals.

These brand core values should also be felt by guests and customers when they come to Nishiwaki to explore the large showroom. From there they have an excellent view through large glass windows into the workshop, and get an impression of its sound, the atmosphere of concentration, and the yarns' lively colours.

The tasteful completion of Tamaki Niime's concept can be found in the room above the showroom, simply called the "tabe room" (eating space). Once in a while, customers can enjoy excellent vegan cuisine here with the team at lunchtime. And, of course, the rice and vegetables are organically grown in the surrounding area.

**tamaki niime**

Fibres from cotton plants after harvest.

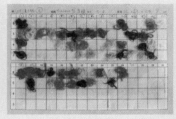
Small colour sample cards of the current batches are placed next to each loom.

A torn weft thread is re-threaded.

玉
木
新
雌

**Tamaki Niime** is the creative head and eponym of her own international clothing brand. She creates her garments in Nishiwaki, Hyōgo Prefecture, with a modern interpretation of *Banshū ori*, fabrics woven from dyed yarn. Her self-chosen name, Niime, in Japanese "new female", is part of the concept and not her original first name.

Tamaki Niime was inspired early on by the idea of one day creating fashion that she would like to wear herself. An encounter with a *Banshū ori* master during her fashion design studies convinced her of the possibilities of this traditional craft. From 2004 she sold her new interpretations of the craft under the name "tamaki niime" in Osaka. Some years later the company moved to Nishiwaki, where the first experiments with old looms began. In 2016, they settled in their present building, a former dye factory. Close to the mountains, water and nature, it is the right size for the approximately twenty-strong team and for Tamaki Niime's ideas for the future.

The former province of Banshū in the southern part of today's

"When I established my brand, I didn't know how it would go. But I believed in myself, that I could do something new, something the people hadn't yet seen. I didn't know what this would be, but I knew that I could create something new. Now I feel really close to reaching that aim. I was also looking for a place where I felt settled and grounded, and finally I have found that place, which is really important for me. So I have become confident. The next step is to try to develop my potential. I want to do a lot of things. But basically, I want to create softness, feathery things, works with new ideas. In ten years, I want to look back and see that I have risen above my possibilities."

Hyōgo Prefecture gave its name to this craftwork about 220 years ago. Influenced by the decorative Nishijin weave from Kyoto, which is over 1,200 years old, *Banshū ori* uses previously dyed yarn, which gives the textile a long-lasting colour and softness, as the fabric itself does not need to be treated after weaving. The combination of colours and patterns results in an infinite variety of woven fabrics.

"My parents had a boutique. When I was a child, we often went to the wholesalers. There I saw large amounts of the same product – I was shocked. At that time I thought: I want to have my own individual clothes. [...] Our works come from experimenting. That makes one of a kind. Sometimes I get inspired by something I worked on yesterday, then I put that inspiration to work today."

All products are washed after weaving.

Checking for weaving faults and sewing on the labels.

View from the shop into the workshop.

**tamaki niime**

**tamaki niime**

tamaki niime

XIII   XIV
XV   XVI

tamaki niime

# Isshū and Shukin Muroya

**Feelings are present,
you just have to allow them,
and preserve them well**

**Isshū and Shukin Muroya**

Two light bulbs softly illuminate the room, panelled with dark wood. Embers in the fireplace warm the room and the hearts of the people while they drink sake together and talk about life. Cats rub against your legs or jump on your lap. As a guest of the calligraphers Isshū and Shukin Muroya, you can enjoy the warm atmosphere of their hospitality in a traditional Japanese half-timbered house.

Classic Japanese calligraphy, often seen in a traditional *tokonoma* room niche and discussed by people attending a tea ceremony, appears very expressive, exciting, as if captured on paper in a moment of inspiration. The much admired expression of the written word, however, is mostly based on traditional calligraphy style. The style is learned by copying virtuoso works, comparable to playing classical music. Right from their university years the two calligraphers felt a conflict with this rigid principle.

"Calligraphy is a picture of your heart, and words are voices of your heart." One day Isshū Muroya found this quote in an old book about Chinese history. It became the key to their joint attitude, and formed the basis of their decision not only to work as free calligraphers but to found their own movement, Jojō calligraphy.

They follow their own convictions, but not without respecting the traditional doctrine. Jojō fits better to their personalities, allowing them to convey emotions and sensual

In winter the snow can even reach up to the first floor of the old farmhouse.

feelings in the expression of their words – the words they encounter in everyday life, which they carefully mull over and from which their works stem. It is more than an attitude: it is their life.

Even if they follow a mutual inspiration and the same impulses, they still differ in their individual ways of working. While Isshū Muroya thinks a lot, makes notes with words and then throws them with a brush onto the paper in a concentrated moment, Shukin Muroya takes the time to fathom out her inner self. Her written, often colourful, sometimes pictorial works can develop analogously to her sensations even during their creation. By opening up the manner of expression, Jojō calligraphy contributes in its own way to a universal exchange with its viewers, especially as it is not always easy to understand the meaning of the Japanese or Chinese characters in full depth.

Their high-quality materials, made by traditional craftspeople, are also called "the Four Friends"

in a Chinese saying. If brush, paper, ink stone and ink go well together, the dialogue between them will have a positive influence on the result. They will become your friends, live with you, breathe the same atmosphere and relax. An ink stone harmonizes with the ink, which is absorbed by the brush and expressively captured in a motif on the paper, which absorbs the ink as intended.

Often it is the subtle differences that make a piece compelling: a particular brush swing, a deeper black, or the end of a curve where the last brush hairs leave the paper.

"What was important to us from the start was that the water we use to make our inks comes out of mountains – natural spring water. The tap water in the cities didn't really do justice. I thought of this quite secretly, and I got really inspired by one particular calligrapher, Tōkō Shinoda, who is now over 100 years old. She has a studio at the bottom of Mount Fuji, and makes her inks from water she collects from snowmelt from Fuji. It did inspire me a lot that people had this idea before me." Isshū Muroya

室谷　一柊・朱琴

Isshū Muroya selects paper for a calligraphic exercise.

Instead of brushes, he also likes to use frayed wisteria twigs.

The calligrapher considers the words he has written.

室谷一柊 **Isshū Muroya** studied classical Japanese calligraphy, but was always looking for a more individual expression of his work. He and his wife founded Jōjō calligraphy, which stands for a free-thinking school in the art of writing. They live on the Noto Peninsula, Ishikawa Prefecture.

室谷朱琴 **Shukin Muroya** learned the art of writing from an early age with renowned traditional calligraphers. Later she also wanted to express things in a way that really spoke from her heart.

The couple met at Kōnan University in Kōbe in the late 1960s and went through life together from that point on. In their search for pure water to use for calligraphy, they first moved to Miyama, Kyoto Prefecture, and then in 2006 to the Noto Peninsula to establish their home and second studio there.

In traditional Japanese calligraphy, one learns to write with brushes, ink and paper through the infinite repetitions of the master's expression. The materials used and even the stroke order of the characters are defined. The founders of Jōjō calligraphy (抒情), an independent movement in this distinguished Japanese way of writing, have offered their alternative since 1981. Both Japanese characters together can be read as "just like carrying water from the well, you carry your feelings". It is an invitation to "freely express your feelings and emotions", which is not always commonplace in Japanese society.

"When I most get inspired is when my five senses are so clear, and I'm so alert, I'm very aware of what's happening. Words pour out of me, and I have the very strong feeling that I want to express this. That's how I make my work. To be able to live in this environment, very close to nature, you have lots of things you have to do to keep up with this style of living, like cutting the grass, and at the end it all leads to making work." Shukin Muroya

"I truly, deeply respect those calligraphers who are in a traditional calligraphy school environment. But it's not the way I want to live and continue my work. When I was a student I read a book in the library. It was an old book about Chinese history, and I found these words saying: 'Calligraphy is a picture of your heart, and words are voices of your heart.' When I met these words I knew this was it. Picture of my heart and voices of my heart, I would like to treasure it and carry on expressing it. Because we are in the calligraphy world, you cannot ignore the traditional side of it, and you shouldn't either. But creative, new styles should also exist parallel to the traditional side." Isshū Muroya

Working on the tatami-covered floor has always been a part of Japanese identity.

All required utensils have their preferred place.

The calligraphers spread out their works on the floor.

# Isshū and Shukin Muroya

室谷　一柊・朱琴

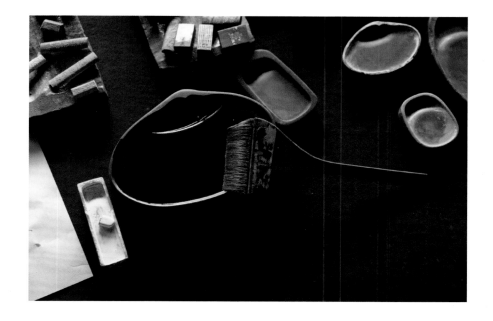

室谷 一柊・朱琴

IX  X
XI  XII

## Isshū and Shukin Muroya

室谷 一柊・朱琴

# Ayane Muroya

**Calligrapher's friends
are aesthetic extensions
of her dancing hands**

**Ayane Muroya**

The vegetation is luxuriant and the sea view is framed by palm trees. On a clear day you can see the snow-covered Hida mountain range, the Japanese Northern Alps, from this idyllic house, a former *minshuku* (family-run guesthouse), overlooking the bay. This beautiful panorama is what Ayane Muroya sees when she opens her studio doors, letting in the sea air and the sound of the waves.

As the daughter of Isshū and Shukin Muroya (see pages 256–265), she grew up observing the practice of calligraphy. She used brushes before using her own chopsticks and continued search-ing for a form of expression in a playful way. Her parents encouraged Ayane to write freely and also to think freely, regardless of rules and traditions. However, confronted with Japan's rigid school system, she felt constricted and restrained. She escaped like the hero of a chil-dren's book she read, setting off for England at the age of thirteen to get to know the outside world, learn the language and go to school.

She stayed for a total of eleven years and came back to Japan with a degree in fine art. She did not actually use calligraphy until her final thesis. Shortly afterwards, aged twenty-three, she realized she was set on the same path as her parents. It was the year of her first solo exhi-bition. In her heart she had always been a calligrapher.

Visiting her parents, Ayane Muroya looks at a calligraphy by her father.

"I think I do more abstract work. I don't really do a lot of writings nowadays unless it's a commissioned work. I guess I combine what I learned during my college time, using sort of traditional calligraphy technique. I just draw lines or circles to create what I want to express. My parents are both quite traditional, and yet, com-pared with the traditional Japanese calligraphy school system, they're alternative, very different, they express how they feel. So I've always been free with words, I'm allowed to do what I want to. I don't even need to use brushes – I could use tree branches to write and draw if I wanted to. That sort of sets me free."

Ayane Muroya now works in a similar way to her mother – so that a work may change even while it is still being created. But sometimes her process is similar to her father's: he only writes his words with a brush when the imagination has matured in an expressive moment. Usually, she herself makes one or two sketches before putting the final result on paper in a creative act, with much feeling and expression, whether this be written words or pictorial or abstract motifs. Like her parents, she stands for the inde-pendent mindset of Jojō calligraphy. She thinks of herself as a second-generation calligrapher, free in mind and methods.

As such, she regularly takes on commissioned work. For example, for the Jardin Paul Bocuse, a gourmet restaurant in Kanazawa, capital of Ishikawa Prefecture, a culinary event using the best ingredients from Noto Peninsula was given a suitable atmosphere by Ayane Muroya's works and calligra-phy menu cards. And a Japanese poet commissioned her to trans-late dozens of his haiku poems into calligraphic works – he had remem-bered seeing her in a television documentary about her parents and herself at the age of seven.

If Ayane Muroya gets stuck with an idea, she sometimes asks her parents for advice. In this way Isshū, Shukin and Ayane Muroya form a small family business in calligraphy.

室谷 文音

I   The spacious house on the coast is surrounded by greenery.
II   Circles (*ensō*) have a positive connotation thanks to their perfection. Incomplete, open circles may represent movement and development.
III   Making some sketches as an exercise.
IV   A painting can be created from the repeated use of characters.

V   The possibility of choosing from different inks, brushes and papers is part of the process.
VI   Calligraphers are always looking for the right material combina-tion for a particular work.
VII   Ayane Muroya with Kaba, her dog.
VIII   Her studio is located in one of the beautiful former guest rooms.

IX   "Gentle Wind", kanji character for wind (*kaze*).
X   A fantastic view of the Japanese Northern Alps in spring.
XI   "Water Spiral", repeating kanji of water (*mizu*) to express the surface of a shining sea. Handmade and dyed *washi* paper by Nigyo Washi, Wajima, Noto.
XII   "I am proposing while holding *sakura* shells in my hand."

Haiku by Suito Ōba, calligraphy by Ayane Muroya. Handmade *washi* paper with embedded pink shells by Nigyo Washi, Wajima, Noto.
XIII   "The Water's Memories." White ink on paper dyed with indigo, handmade by Ayane Muroya.

Ink is ground with water until the right shade of black is achieved.

The making of calligraphy is very contemplative work.

She achieves expressive forms with wide brushes and a lot of practice.

室谷文音 **Ayane Muroya** is a free calligrapher who lives and works on the coast of the Noto Peninsula and for some time in Germany each year. The daughter of Isshū and Shukin Muroya, she was born in Kyoto Prefecture, and expressed herself with calligraphy from an early age.

She moved to England when she was a teenager, where she graduated in fine art from Central Saint Martins College of Art and Design in London in 2003. Just one year later her first solo exhibition took place in a gallery in Kyoto, followed by exhibitions in London, Liverpool, Tokyo, Osaka, Kōbe and, of course Noto. In 2008 she established her atelier, "Tokarin", where she also offers calligraphy workshops.
    Calligraphy in Japan is known as the "way of writing" (*shodō*). Styles and characters were originally taken from Chinese calligraphy. Through the addition of the Japanese syllable fonts katakana and in particular hiragana, home-grown styles developed over time. It was practised and refined by Buddhist monks, at the imperial court, and later also

"From the outside our life looks a bit crazy, and it is a bit of struggle to go back and forth. But for me, here in Japan, I have enough space to do work. Everything, like working on the floor, sitting on the floor, helps me to get into work very naturally. When I try to do that in Berlin, I have to prepare more, and I think my brain doesn't really adjust so well to that. For me, it's also very important to go back and forth to Europe to recharge myself. When I'm in Japan for a long time, I become more sort of restricted within myself. I need to see and feel and be in that environment to realize that it's just a part of the world, and the normality here won't necessarily be correct in a different culture."

by officials from the samurai class. Traditional calligraphy follows relatively narrow guidelines as to the materials, words and spellings that should be used. A second-generation calligrapher, Ayane Muroya works according to the ideas of Jojō calligraphy, an independent movement established by her parents (see page 260).

"Once you start going to school you have to have Japanese lessons, plus calligraphy lessons. And it was the first time I realized that there are given ways to write kanji – it's stroke one, stroke two, and so on, the correct way to do it. It was really shocking to find out that somebody had already decided this. My parents taught me freely, so I was able to draw from anywhere, any direction."

Paperweights (*bunchin*) hold down the sheet while writing.

Usually everything is accessible from the cushion.

Seashells, driftwood and other beach-combed objects are found in the house.

**Ayane Muroya**

室谷　文音

IV V
VI VII

**Ayane Muroya**

室谷 文音

"A journey means
that you have more
than one home after
you come back."

From a letter by Isshū Muroya

## Nigara Forging

二唐刃物鍛造所

› 14

Iron production was an important economic factor in the Tsugaru region around the Iwaki volcano as far back as the Heian period (794–1185). At the end of the Sengoku period (c. 1467–1590) the feudal lord Ōura Tamenobu conquered several castles of the Nanbu clan in the region of Tsugaru, and renamed himself Tsugaru Tamenobu. After the Battle of Sekigahara in 1600, he consolidated his holdings and began construction of Hirosaki Castle as the centre of the Hirosaki Domain over which the Tsugaru clan ruled. A strong black-smithing craft with more than 100 forges began to flourish. The workshop of Nigara Forging, with one room each for forging and grinding, has been located in the metal district (kinzoku-machi) of Hirosaki, Aomori Prefecture, since 1975.
› nigara.jp

## Suzuki Morihisa Studio

鈴木盛久工房

› 24

Morioka, Iwate Prefecture, developed over the centuries into a centre for iron casting because of its rich local resources. The locally mined iron sand could be smelted to a high standard. The river sand required for the ornaments in the moulds was also found locally with the confluence of three rivers. Clay for the moulds, charcoal for firing and urushi lacquer for the protective coating were all obtained in the area. All the essential requirements for casting high-quality iron works were met. For many iron founders in the country, this was reason enough to settle in the region. Since 1885, Suzuki Morihisa's workshop has been located in an area home to numerous craft workshops, after a big fire in the city destroyed the company's former workshop buildings.
› suzukimorihisa.com

## Shimatani Syouryu Koubou

昇龍工房 シマタニ

› 34

At the beginning of the Edo period (1603–1868), the local ruling Maeda clan was able to persuade some excellent metal casters to settle in its domain. Initially they manufactured cast-iron pots and kettles, but soon they also made brassware and cast-bronze Buddhist altar fittings, which were in demand throughout Japan. This is the origin of Takaoka dōki (Takaoka copperware and bronze casting), which today represents 90 per cent of all such products in Japan. The craft of hammered orin gongs developed in parallel to the specialization in Buddhist altar fittings. Shimatani's workshop rooms are located on the ground floor of two buildings in a residential area in Takaoka, Toyama Prefecture, separated by a narrow street.
› syouryu.com

## Masami Mizuno

水野正美

› 44

During the Wadō ("Japanese copper") era (708–715), important copper resources in today's Saitama Prefecture were discovered, which led to the minting of copper coins, forming Japan's first currency. Japan became one of the most important copper producers in Asia through improved metal production processes. During the Edo period (1603–1868), Tsubame in Niigata Prefecture developed as a traditional region for hammer-cast copperware (tsuiki dōki), and remains an important centre for metal processing today. The city of Nagoya is the fourth-largest industrial centre in Japan and the capital of Aichi Prefecture. Masami Mizuno's studio is located in a beautiful old house in a central but quiet residential area.
› sites.google.com/site/mizuno033

## Chiyozuru Sadahide Studio

千代鶴貞秀工房

› 54

Miki in Hyōgo Prefecture is the best-known city in Japan for the production of carpentry tools. The presence of iron oxide in the mountains of Chūgoku to the west and cinnabar at Mount Tanjō (Niuyama) to the east caused the Yamato Imperial Court to take direct control of the region. At the end of the Sengoku period, the Age of Warring States (c. 1467–1590), carpenters gathered in Miki to rebuild the heavily damaged town. With them, the industry for hand-forged carpentry tools flourished. In 1996, the Japanese government recognized Banshū Miki forged blades as "national traditional crafts", specifically saws, irons, chisels, planes (kanna), and craft knives (kogatana). The two workshops of Chiyozuru Sadahide are located in the neighbouring cities of Miki and Ono.
› chiyozurusadahide.jp

## Kobayashi Shikki

小林漆器

› 66

The Tsugaru nuri lacquer style originated in the late seventeenth century during the reign of the local Tsugaru clan. Over a long period, only valuable objects were made for the rulers and for upper class. Samurai families picked up the craft in the late Edo period. The elegant and durable lacquerware was later made available to a wider public in the Meiji era (1868–1912). A large number of everyday objects were now provided with Tsugaru nuri surfaces. The town of Hirosaki, Aomori Prefecture, is located close to Mount Iwaki, where lacquer trees are cultivated. The modern two-storey workshop building and showroom of Kobayashi Shikki is located next to the family home in a residential area near the castle of Hirosaki.
› kobayashishikki.com

## Junko Yashiro

八代淳子

› 74

Junko Yashiro does not feel that she belongs to either a classical style or a traditional region for urushi lacquer work such as Wajima nuri, Aizu nuri or Kishū shikki. But she wanted to escape the narrowness of Tokyo and to live in the midst of the Karuizawa forests, which she knew from her childhood holidays. Since the Meiji era (1868–1912), Tokyo residents have used the area in Nagano Prefecture as a summer resort. The modern architect-designed house includes an annexe for her woodworking studio. A second studio for urushi work is attached to the living rooms. The house and studio appear both Japanese modern and European at the same time.
› junko-yashiro.net

## Yanase Washi

やなせ和紙

› 84

As a former producer of paper money, the region of Echizen, in today's Fukui Prefecture, established close ties with the imperial court and the shogunate at an early stage. The famous papermaker Heizaburō Iwano (1878–1960) was able to raise the quality of papers for nihonga (Japanese-style painting) to become independent of Chinese suppliers, which also led to orders for papers for sliding doors. Echizen's Goka area, a cluster of five small villages, is currently home to about thirty traditional papermakers. Based on centuries of tradition and constant innovation, the region has earned itself an excellent reputation for its wide variety of paper production. The spacious workshop and dwelling of Yanase Washi is located in the middle of a small side valley, among other private buildings and workshops.
› washicco.jp

## Atelier Kawahira

工房かわひら

› 94

When long ago the local rulers in Sekishū region (part of today's Shimane Prefecture) encouraged the farmers to produce paper from kōzo fibres in winter, a paper was created that is known today as *Sekishū washi*. Compared to the large urban regions of Kōbe, Okayama and Hiroshima, Shimane Prefecture is located on the less developed side of the main Japanese island of Honshū. The local papermaking craftsmanship has not yet disappeared as there are few industrial jobs in the region. The workshop of Atelier Kawahira is located next to the family home. In an old wooden building, the fibres are boiled and beaten and the sheets dried. The scooping and cutting of the paper takes place in a newer building across the street.
› kaminokunikara.jp

## Take Kobo Once

竹工房オンセ

› 104

Bamboo basketry from Beppu (*Beppu take zaiku*) is mainly based on the madake bamboo (*Phyllostachys bambusoides*), which is widely available in Ōita Prefecture. In the Muromachi period (1338–1573), plaited bamboo goods were mainly distributed by travelling hawkers, with a great demand being sparked by visitors to the famous hot springs in the Edo period. What started out as an additional form of income for farmers developed into a separate craft branch. In his search for land for organic farming, Masato Takae found a property in the mountains above Beppu. However, instead of planting crops, he built a two-storey log house with friends over a period of several years. For the studio they built a second log cabin on the site.
› take-once.com

## Hajime Nakatomi

中臣一

› 114

Ōita Prefecture is a nationwide centre for arts and crafts related to the fascinating bamboo plant. Thanks to ideal conditions about 40 per cent of Japan's bamboo groves can be found here on the southern island of Kyūshū. Hajime Nakatomi's studio is located in an old comprehensive school outside the centre of Taketa city. The former music classroom offers him ample space to work and plenty of daylight. Since 2012, and as part of the TSG Project (Taketa Sogo Gakuin, Taketa Comprehensive School), the local administration has made the premises available as artists' studios in their efforts to re-establish bamboo craft in Taketa. Together with other bamboo artists, Hajime Nakatomi cultivates his own bamboo grove in the surroundings.
› h-nakatomi.com

## BUAISOU

› 126

When the Yoshino River in Tokushima region was not yet bordered by dikes, the flat valley bottom was regularly flooded by heavy rainfall during the typhoon season. As this coincided with the rice harvesting period, the area was not suitable for rice cultivation. The indigo plant, which was otherwise difficult to cultivate, proved ideal for these fertile areas of land. In this way, today's Tokushima Prefecture became in former times the most important indigo producer in Japan. The river has long been tamed, but the cultivation of Japanese indigo has remained. It is still the basis for natural indigo dye. BUAISOU's workshop is located near the Yoshino River in a former stable surrounded by fields and greenhouses.
› buaisou-i.com

## ISSO

一草

› 136

Tokushima Prefecture is known throughout the country for the production of Awa indigo, named after the ancient name of the Tokushima region. In the Azuchi-Momoyama period (1573–1603), the local lords of the Hachisuka clan spread indigo cultivation in their territory. In the Edo period (1603–1868), Tokushima indigo dominated most of the Japanese market. At the end of the Meiji period (1868–1912) the market collapsed, as cheap indigo was increasingly imported from India, while synthetic indigo was developed in Germany around 1900. Tokiko Kajimoto's studio is located in a residential area in Tokushima south of the Yoshino River. In the surrounding area, the narrow architect-designed house by Shinji Tomita is only noticeable at second glance.
› awa-ai.com

## Tree to Green

› 144

The narrow and tortuous Kiso Valley in Nagano and Gifu Prefecture is home to large quantities of the hinoki and sawara cypress, Japanese thuja (nezuko), umbrella pine (kōyamaki) and hiba (asunaro) – sometimes called the "five sacred trees of Kiso" – and some sugi (Japanese cedar). The cold winters of the region let the trees grow slowly and with a qualitatively better, denser structure. The wood of each tree species has special characteristics that have long been used in Japan by specialized craftspeople for certain products. The head office of Tree to Green is located in Tokyo, while the company has its own workshop not far from the town of Kiso in a side valley. Kosegi Mokko's workshop is located in the southern Kiso Valley in Nojiri village.
› treetogreen.com

## TATEMOKU

楯
木
工
製
作
所

› 156

Many wood-processing companies in the Kiso region use wood from the local forests according to their natural characteristics. Kiso hinoki has finer wood fibres thanks to the local climate conditions, which predestines it for use in *kumiko* works. The flexibility of the fibres is of great importance for the thinly sawn strips. TATEMOKU's workshop is located above the Kiso River, at a bend in the Kiso Valley to the west, just a few hundred metres from the famous historic postal town of Tsumago. Today's tourist destination used to be an important postal station on the Nakasendō route between the former centres of Edo and Kyoto (see right). The company runs a store there selling woodwork from its own production.
› tatemoku.jp

## Okekazu

桶
数

› 164

In addition to the excellent quality of the wood grown here and the handcrafted products made from it, the topographical location is one of the reasons for the reputation of the Kiso region. The western part of the famous old postal road Nakasendō ("central mountain route") runs through the valley. It was an important connection between the capital Edo (today's Tokyo) and the old imperial city of Kyoto during the Edo period. Okekazu's workshop was built in the mid-1990s. The building has a showroom and a workshop for the smaller buckets and vats. A second workshop building in a side valley is mainly used for the production of large barrels and solid wood bathtubs.
› okekazu.jp

## Yamaichi Ogura Rokuro Crafts

ロクロ工芸所
ヤマイチ小椋

› 174

During the Edo period (1603–1868), the Owari clan that ruled the Kiso region promoted forestry. Plain bowls and trays made at the beginning of the eighteenth century found their way to Nagoya and Osaka. From then, *Nagiso rokuro zaiku*, with its containers turned from solid wood, started to earn the reputation that it still enjoys today. It is based in particular on the extraordinary sense of local artisans for their material. Today, only six turners manufacture the local wood products from Kiso. Yamaichi Ogura Rokuro Crafts operates its workshop at the end of a small side valley in the Kiso region, Nagano Prefecture. The wood yard and some smaller workshop buildings are located behind the substantial main building with its large showroom.
› yamaichi-rokuro.com

## OTA MOKKO

› 184

In the Edo period, Odawara Castle controlled important sections of the Tōkaidō ("eastern sea route"), the old postal and trade route that connected the historical Edo, residence of the Tokugawa Shogunate, with the old imperial city of Kyoto. Within sight of the castle is the old woodworking district of Odawara. Wood turners in the local *kijibiki* style are said to have worked here since the Heian period (794–1185). Later, other wood-based handicrafts such as Odawara lacquerwork, puzzle boxes (*karakuri zaiku*), wood inlay or marquetry (*moku zogan*) and wooden toys were also produced. Ken Ota runs his *yosegi zaiku* workshop and store under the name OTA MOKKO, together with his wife, in the old woodworking district in a former noodle factory.
› ota-mokko.com

## Kazuto Yoshikawa

吉川 和人

› 194

More than 37 million people live in the greater metropolitan area of Tokyo (as of 2015), making it the most populous agglomeration in the world. Local artists and artisans have to shoulder the high cost of living, but the flip side is that they find exhibition opportunities and many potential buyers for their own works. Moreover, Tokyo has been an important centre for various traditional crafts such as weaving, dyeing and glasswork since the Edo era or before. Kazuto Yoshikawa runs his wood workshop in the middle of the Setagaya district in Tokyo, renting a part of a local carpenter's workshop. He lives with his family not far away in the same neighbourhood.
› kazutoyoshikawa.com

## Koichi Onozawa

小野澤弘一

› 204

Tochigi Prefecture is known in the world of ceramics for the original ceramic styles *Mashiko yaki* (Mashiko ware), *Koisago yaki* and *Mikamo yaki*. The region around Nakagawa, and especially Daigo, a nearby town in Ibaraki Prefecture, is also known for extracting high quality *urushi* from local lacquer trees. Cuts are made in the bark of trees aged about twelve years and the sap secreted is collected during the summer season. The trees will die afterwards, but after being cut down cleanly at the root, new sprouts will grow again the next year. Koichi Onozawa has been involved in the local regeneration efforts of urushi trees by a dedicated nonprofit organization. His studio in a small warehouse and his residence are located in a side valley of the Naka River, near the city of Nakagawa.
› koichionozawa.com

## Shozo Michikawa

道川省三

› 214

Northeast of Nagoya lies the city of Seto, Aichi Prefecture. It is one of the so-called Six Ancient Kilns ("Rokkoyō"), and also one of the most characteristic ceramic cities in Japan. High-quality clay is still mined in many places around the town, and is processed by countless small and large potteries and manufacturers of everyday ceramics. Every year in September the Setomono Matsuri takes place, a ceramics festival that attracts thousands of visitors. As a studio, Shozo Michikawa uses a small room in an old tile factory at the northern edge of Seto. He was given the chance many years ago to rent the place together with other ceramicists, where they can also share a gas kiln.
› shozo-michikawa.com
› icaf-sasama.com

## Toru Hatta

八田亨

› 226

Osaka is the third largest city in Japan, after Tokyo and Yokohama, and a traditional trading centre. Originally called Naniwa, it is also known as a birthplace of Sue ceramics (*sueki*). Initially used only for funerary and ritual objects, these dark-grey unglazed pieces can be traced back to early trade relationships with Korea. Sue pottery was produced in Japan and Korea especially during the Kofun, Nara and Heian periods (*c.* 300–1185) and many characteristic ceramic styles in Japan developed subsequently. Toru Hatta lives with his family in Tondabayashi, southeast of Osaka, in an area of beautiful old town houses. He has a small pottery studio in an extension of their newly built house. His wood-fired kiln is located on the site of a second studio in nearby Sakai.
› hattatoru.com

## Kasamori | 000

笠盛 — 000

› 236

The city of Kiryū, Gunma Prefecture, developed into a centre of Japanese sericulture and textile production from the Nara period (710–794). Centuries later, Tokugawa Ieyasu even used white silk flags from Kiryū in the decisive Battle of Sekigahara in 1600. In the following Edo period (1603–1868), refined weaving technologies from Nishijin, Kyoto, were introduced. The industry developed rapidly, and soon it was said: "For the West it is Nishijin, for the East it is Kiryū." The significance of this craft for the town can be seen today by the many sawtooth roofs typical of the production buildings. Kasamori produces in an old wooden building and a modern annexe, which both have the characteristic roofs.
› kasamori.co.jp
› 000-triple.com

## tamaki niime

› 246

In the traditional *Banshū ori* craft, yarn dyeing precedes weaving. Coming from the local mountains, the required soft, clear water was always available in Nishiwaki, Hyōgo Prefecture. A dyeing craft developed that supplied yarns for local farming families who used them to weave *Banshū ori* fabrics according to defined specifications. The modern looms turned it into a locally rooted industrial craft. The large white workshop of tamaki niime near the city of Nishiwaki is part of the building complex of a former dyeing plant. Here all textiles of the brand are produced, sewn and presented in a large showroom. The cotton fields growing cotton for some of their own yarn and the rice and vegetable fields for the "tabe room" are nearby.
› niime.jp

## Isshū and Shukin Muroya

一柊・朱琴
室谷

› 256

The Noto Peninsula, in the north of Ishikawa Prefecture, which extends far into the Japanese Sea, captivates above all with its natural richness and rural surroundings. The remoteness and rugged topography mean that there are only a few built-up areas, but all the more forests with their dense greenery. Isshū and Shukin Muroya chose their previous residence in the rural environment of Kyoto in order to be able to work with the good natural spring water. The same applies to Noto, but they also appreciate it as a wonderful place of inspiration. The couple reside right on the edge of the forest, in a beautiful old farmhouse with a view of a small valley. Thanks to the high location near the Japanese Sea, several metres of snow can fall here in winter.

## Ayane Muroya

室谷
文音

› 266

Although calligraphy uses only handcrafted products, it has no regional associations. Rather, the high-quality handmade papers, brushes, ink and ink stones found their way to the calligraphers, who lived especially in Buddhist monasteries and in the long-established cultural centres of Kyoto and Edo (Tokyo). The Noto Peninsula is blessed with great natural resources. Its excellent water quality harmonizes well with the special calligraphy ink. Local papermakers appreciate it for making paper of good quality, which in turn is used in calligraphy. Ayane Muroya lives with her husband in a former *minshuku* (family-run bed-and-breakfast accommodation) that offers plenty of space for her work and an inspiring environment right on the coast.
› ateliertokarin.com

## Acknowledgments

Our deepest thanks to Ayane Muroya, Paul Muthers and Hiroki Iwasa, without whom this project would not have been possible, to Junko Kawashima and Yuika Kubo of JETRO, and to our families and friends for their continual support. To Alexa Vachon, Walter Hellmann and Kirsty Seymour-Ure, as well as to Lucas Dietrich and Fleur Jones of Thames & Hudson for their advice, and special thanks to Kengo Kuma for his foreword. But especially to all the craftspeople and artists, their families and staff members who have shared their thoughts and hearts with us (in order of visit): Shozo and Masae Michikawa; Nori, Miyoko, Yoshinori Sakai and Tamaki Niime; Isao and Masao Kawahira and Hamada City Office; Masato and Etsuko Takae, Nobuhiro Miyamoto, Noriko and Naoki Yoshida; Hajime Nakatomi, Toru Kato; Tokiko and Yudai Kajimoto; Kyoko Nishimoto and BUAISOU's team; Iwao Kanki and Naoki Morita; Toru Hatta, Yuki Kondo, Ninni Mäklin and Emi Uda; Yanase family, Echizen Paper and Culture Museum; Masami Mizuno, Sayako Kidokoro, Ian Orgias and Mitsue Iwakoshi of Analogue Life; Junko and Takeshi Yashiro, Miki Mita; Yasutoshi Kasahara, Yoichi Katakura; Koichi and Noriko Onozawa, Yasuka Sato; Kobayashi family; Shiiko Kumagai and Shigeo Suzuki; Go and Toshihisa Yoshizawa; Kazuto Yoshikawa; Ken and Umi Ota, Mariko Harigai; Takanori and Lena Kosegi, Hideo Kosegi and his wife; Kesao and Takumi Ito; Kazuo Ogura; Toshihiko Tate; Yoshinori and Kumekazu Shimatani; and to Isshū and Shukin Muroya.

## Additional images

Nigara Forging: p. 19 top; Suzuki Morihisa Studio: p. 29, p. 30 top left, right, bottom left; Chiyozuru Sadahide Studio: p. 59; Jihei Kunisaki: p. 99, from: *Kamisuki Chohoki*, 1798; Take Kobo Once: p. 109; Yūsuke Nishibe: p. 119; Kyoko Nishimoto / BUAISOU: p. 130 top left, middle, p. 135; Siebold and Zuccarini: p. 149, from: *Flora Japonica*, 1835–70; Tree to Green: p. 155 bottom left, right; Nacása & Partners Inc. / Tree to Green: p. 159; TATEMOKU: p. 160 bottom left, right; Miho Urushiwaki / Ryu Kosaka of A.N.D.: p. 169; Unknown: p. 179; Yamaichi Ogura Rokuro Crafts: p. 180 top middle; Kazuto Yoshikawa: p. 199, p. 200 top left, right, bottom; Yoshinori Seguchi: p. 219 top and bottom; Alessandra Vinci: p. 219 middle; Toru Hatta: p. 229; Kasamori: p. 240 top, bottom middle; tamaki niime: p. 255 top; Isshū and Shukin Muroya: p. 259

Every effort has been made to contact copyright owners for material reproduced in this book.
Please contact Thames & Hudson with any queries.

p. 2 Koichi Onozawa prepares clay for his works.
p. 7 The surface of a forged plane blade is worked by Chiyozuru Sadahide III.
p. 11 Near Nakano, Nagano Prefecture.

p. 12 On the west coast of northern Japan.
p. 276–7 On the north coast of Noto Peninsula.
p. 278 During Tomobata Matsuri, a local festival, in the bay of Ogi, Noto Peninsula.

# Index

First published in the United Kingdom
in 2020 by Thames & Hudson Ltd,
181A High Holborn, London WC1V 7QX

First published in 2020 in the United
States of America by Thames & Hudson
Inc., 500 Fifth Avenue, New York,
New York 10110

Reprinted 2021

*Craftland Japan* © 2020
Thames & Hudson Ltd, London
Design © 2020 Uwe Röttgen and
Katharina Zettl
Text and photography © 2020
Uwe Röttgen and Katharina Zettl

British Library Cataloguing-in-
Publication Data
A catalogue record for this book is
available from the British Library

Library of Congress Control Number
2019953322

ISBN 978-0-500-29534-2

Printed and bound in China by C&C Offset
Printing Co Ltd

Be the first to know about our new releases,
exclusive content and author events by visiting
**thamesandhudson.com**
**thamesandhudsonusa.com**
**thamesandhudson.com.au**

FSC
www.fsc.org
MIX
Paper from
responsible sources
**FSC® C008047**